# Nicky Epstein
## ❀Crochet for Dolls

# Nicky Epstein

## Crochet for Dolls

### 25 Fun, Fabulous Outfits
### for 18-Inch Dolls

Nicky Epstein Books

AN IMPRINT OF
SIXTH&SPRING
BOOKS
NEW YORK

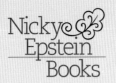

AN IMPRINT OF SIXTH&SPRING BOOKS
161 AVENUE OF THE AMERICAS, NEW YORK NY 10013
SIXTHANDSPRINGBOOKS.COM

EDITORIAL DIRECTOR
JOY AQUILINO

DEVELOPMENTAL
EDITOR
LISA SILVERMAN

ART DIRECTOR
DIANE LAMPHRON

YARN EDITOR
CHRISTINA BEHNKE

EDITORIAL
ASSISTANT/STYLIST
JOHANNA LEVY

INSTRUCTIONS
EDITORS
JO BRANDON
STEPHANIE MRSE
SANDI PROSSER

TECHNICAL
ILLUSTRATIONS
KAREN MANTHEY
LISA SILVERMAN

DESIGN/ART
PRODUCTION
DEBORAH GRISORIO

STILL PHOTOGRAPHY
JACK DEUTSCH

PROP STYLIST
DIANE LAMPHRON

VICE PRESIDENT
TRISHA MALCOLM

PUBLISHER
CARRIE KILMER

PRODUCTION
MANAGER
DAVID JOINNIDES

PRESIDENT
ART JOINNIDES

CHAIRMAN
JAY STEIN

Cataloging-in-Publication data
is available from the Library of Congress.

ISBN: 978-1-936096-59-6


MANUFACTURED IN CHINA

1 3 5 7 9 10 8 6 4 2

First Edition

# Contents

Introduction 10

The Crochet for Dolls Collection 13

Extras and Resources 117

   A Little Bit of Bling 118

   Sweets for the Sweet 119

   Glossary & Techniques 120

   Yarn Resources 123

Index 124

Acknowledgments 126

Afternoon Tea
*page 14*

Get Your Kicks
*page 18*

Give It a Whirl
*page 23*

Southern Belle
*page 27*

Fit for a Fiesta
*page 30*

A Night at the Opera
*page 34*

Hip to Be Square
*page 39*

Daisy Mays
*page 44*

Wildflower
*page 47*

Slip into Sleepytime
*page 51*

Circus of Color
*page 54*

Royal Princess
*page 59*

Dressed Up in Daisies
*page 64*

Striped Safari
*page 66*

Irish Eyes
*page 71*

Pretty as a Picture
*page 75*

Wrapped in Ruffles
*page 79*

Cowl and Critters
*page 82*

Wise Owl Hat
*page 84*

Butterfly Hat
*page 85*

Meow Kitty Hat
*page 86*

Candy Couture
*page 87*

Floral Beauty
*page 91*

Let It Snow
*page 94*

Walking on Sunshine
*page 97*

Checkmate
*page 101*

Go-go Girl
*page 104*

Budding Beauty
*page 107*

Arctic Angel
*page 112*

# Grab Bag

Mix and match these adorable purse designs
with your favorite outfits.

**PRETTY AS A PICTURE**
*page 75*

**GIVE IT A WHIRL**
*page 23*

**CIRCUS OF COLOR**
*page 54*

**ARCTIC ANGEL**
*page 112*

**GO-GO GIRL**
*page 104*

**CANDY
COUTURE**
*page 87*

**ROYAL
PRINCESS**
*page 59*

**WALKING ON SUNSHINE**
*page 97*

**CHECKMATE**
*page 101*

# Introduction

Over the years, whenever I've released a new
knitting book, I've heard crocheters say "I wish this were
a crochet book"—even though I have written a few.
Well, crocheters . . . I've got you covered!

When I created *Nicky Epstein Knits For Dolls*, I also designed 25 exclusive crochet
pieces for 18-inch dolls, which I hope the single-needle crowd will love.

I love dolls—who doesn't—and have always found great joy knitting
and crocheting for them. Now that 18-inch dolls are soaring in popularity, they
need great-looking fashions, and I've designed for the dolls as I would for
the little girls (and big girls) who cherish them.

The garments in this book range from casual to high style and are easy
and fun, whether you're crocheting for your dolls or for a special
"little one" with whom you might share the experience.

Although I am a better knitter than a crocheter, I love crochet and enjoyed
designing these pieces, as I hope you will enjoy making them.
The bulk of the designs were crocheted by my dear friend and fantastic crocheter
Jo Brandon. She always says, "If I can make them, anyone can."

I hope *Crochet for Dolls* reassures crocheters everywhere that I have not
forgotten you, and that we belong to a special sisterhood (or brotherhood),
whether we use one needle or two. Happy crocheting!

NICKY EPSTEIN

The Crochet
for Dolls
Collection

# Afternoon Tea

Dainty scalloped petals on the skirt and sleeves make a ladylike dress perfect for a tea party.

## MATERIALS

- 1 .35oz/10g ball (each approx 77yd/70m) of Presencia *Finca Perlé 8* (cotton) each in #599 pale blue (A), #387 light blue (B), #197 blue (C), #547 dark blue (D), and #900 blanco (E)
- Size B/1 (2.25mm) hook OR SIZE TO OBTAIN GAUGE
- 3 buttons, ⅜"/1cm diameter
- Stitch markers

## GAUGE

6 scallops and 12 scallop rows = 4"/10cm over layered scallop pat using size B/1 (2.25mm) hook.
*Take time to check gauge.*

## LAYERED SCALLOP PATTERN

First row of scallops:
**ROW 1** *Ch 5, sk next 4 sts, sl st in next st; rep from * to end, turn.
**ROW 2** Ch 1, *[1 sc, 2 hdc, 3 dc, ch 1, 3dc, 2 hdc, 1 sc] in next ch-5 sp; rep from * to end, turn.
Continued base:
**ROW 3** Ch 3 (counts as 1 dc), dc in next sc of base row 2 and in each sc to end, turn.
**ROW 4** Ch 1, sc in 1st dc and each dc to end, turn.
2nd row of scallops:
Rep rows 1 and 2 of first row of scallops.
Continued base:
**ROW 5** Ch 3 (counts as 1 dc), dc in next sc of base row 4 and in each sc to end, turn.
**ROW 6** Ch 3 (counts as 1 dc), dc in next dc and in each dc to end, turn.
**ROW 7** Ch 1, sc in 1st dc and each dc to end. Fasten off.
3rd and 4th row of scallops:
With WS facing, attach yarn to right-hand edge of foundation ch (so all scallops are RS facing).
**ROWS 8–14** Rep rows 1–7 once more. Fasten off.

## BODICE PATTERN STITCH

**ROW 1** Dc in 2nd ch from hook, *sc in next ch, dc in next ch; rep from * across.
**ROW 2** Sc in dc, dc in each sc across.
Rep row 2 for bodice pat st.

## NOTES

**1)** Skirt of dress is worked in one piece from waist to lower hem.
**2)** Bodice of dress is worked in one piece from waist to shoulder.

## SKIRT

BASE
With A, ch 76.
**ROW 1** Dc in 2nd ch from hook and in each ch to end, turn—75 sts.
**ROW 2** Ch 1, 1 sc in each dc to end, turn.

BEG SCALLOP PATTERN
Work rows 1–14 of layered scallop pattern in each color: A, B, C, D, end final row with row 2. Fasten off.

## LAYERED SCALLOP PATTERN

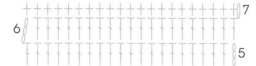

continued base

second row of scallops

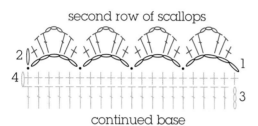

continued base

first row of scallops

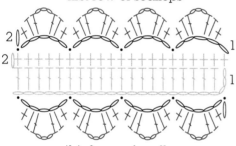

third row of scallops

## Stitch Key

- • slip stitch (sl st)
- ◠ chain (ch)
- ✛ single crochet (sc)
- ⊤ double crochet (dc)
- ◖ draw up a loop

16

## TOP

With E, ch 75.

**ROW 1 (RS)** Dc in 2nd ch from hook, *sc in next ch, dc in next ch; rep from * to last ch, sc in last ch, turn—74 sts.

**ROW 2** Ch 1, *sc in next dc, dc in next sc; rep from * across, turn. Rep row 2 until piece measures 1"/2.5cm, end with a WS row.

## DIVIDE FOR FRONTS AND BACK

**NEXT ROW (RS)** Pat 18 sts for left back, place marker #1, pat 8 sts for left underarm, place marker #2, pat 22 sts for front, place marker #3, pat 8 sts for right underarm, place marker #4, pat to end, turn.

## RIGHT BACK

**NEXT ROW (WS)** Pat to marker 4, turn and work pattern for 2½"/6.5cm, end with RS facing. Sl st across 5 sts, work pat on rem 13 sts for 1"/2.5cm. Fasten off.

## LEFT BACK

With WS facing, attach yarn at marker #1. Work as for right back, reversing sl st 5 sts.

## FRONT

With WS facing, attach yarn at marker #3, work pat to marker #2, turn. Cont in pat for 1"/2.5cm, end with RS facing.

**NEXT ROW** Pat 8 sts, sl st across next 6 sts, pat next 8 sts, turn. Cont working on last 8 sts for 4 rows. Fasten off. With RS facing, attach yarn to corresponding 8 sts of RS and cont working on 8 sts for 4 rows. Fasten off.

## FINISHING

Sew shoulder seams.

## NECK AND BACK OPENING EDGING

With RS facing, attach A to lower edge of center left back. Work in sc evenly along center left back edge, work 2 sc in corner, work in sc evenly along neck edge to center right back edge, work 2 sc in corner, work in sc evenly along center right back edge. Fasten off.

## RIGHT ARMHOLE EDGING

With RS facing, attach A at center of underarm between markers #3 and #4.

**RND 1** Work 41 sc evenly around opening, join with a sl st to first sc.

**RND 2** Sc in next 9 sc, [ch 5, sk 5 sts, sl st in next sc] 4 times, sc in each st to end of rnd.

**RND 3** Sc in next 9 sc, [(sc, 2hdc, 3dc, ch 1, 3dc, 2hdc, sc) in next ch-5 sp] 4 times, sc in each st to end of rnd, join with a sl st to first sc. Fasten off.

Rep for left armhole edging, attaching A at center of underarm between markers #1 and #2.

Join bodice to skirt using sc and A. Sew skirt center back seam. Sew buttons to RS of right back bodice. ✿

# Get Your Kicks

A brightly striped playset with jacket, capri pants, and visor has her ready to take the field in style.

## MATERIALS
- 1 1¾oz/50g ball (each approx 181yd/165m) of Grignasco *Champagne* (merino/silk) each in #308 gray (A) and #3905 yellow (B)
- One each sizes C/2 (2.75mm) and D/3 (3.25mm) hooks OR SIZE TO OBTAIN GAUGE
- Approx 6"/15cm of flexible wire (for visor)
- One small snap
- One 4"/10cm separating zipper
- Thread and sewing needle (for zipper)

## GAUGE
20 sts and 24 rows = 4"/10cm using size D/3 (3.25mm) hook.
*Take time to check gauge.*

## STITCH GLOSSARY
**BP TR (BACK POST TREBLE CROCHET)** Yo 2 times, insert hook from back to front around the post of the corresponding stitch below, yarn over and pull up loop, [yarn over, draw through two loops on hook] 3 times.

## JACKET BACK
With size D/3 (3.25mm) hook and B, ch 31.
**ROW 1** Hdc in 2nd ch from hook and in each ch across, turn—30 sts.
**ROWS 2–13** Ch 2, hdc in each hdc to end of row, turn.

### ARMHOLE SHAPING
**ROW 14** Ch 2, hdc2tog, hdc in each st to last 2 hdc, hdc2tog, turn.
Rep last row 4 times more—20 sts.

### RIGHT NECK AND SHOULDER SHAPING
**ROW 19** Ch 2, hdc in next 4 hdc, turn.
Rep last row 3 times more.
**ROW 23** Sl st across first 4 hdc and across neck edge to last 4 hdc, hdc in each of last 4 hdc, turn.

### LEFT NECK AND SHOULDER SHAPING
**ROW 24** Ch 2, hdc in next 4 hdc, turn.
Rep last row twice more. Fasten off.

## LEFT FRONT
With size D/3 (3.25mm) hook and B, ch 17.
Work following chart 1 in hdc, using B and A as directed for diagonal pattern.

## RIGHT FRONT
Work the same as left side, using chart 2.
Sew jacket fronts to jacket back at shoulders.

## SLEEVES
With size D/3 (3.25mm) hook and B, attach yarn at start of armhole on right front, ch 1, work 13 hdc along front armhole edge to shoulder, work 2 hdc at shoulder, work 13 hdc along back armhole edge, turn—28 hdc.
**ROW 1** Ch 2, hdc2tog, hdc in each st to last 2 sts, hdc2tog, turn.
**ROW 2** Ch 2, hdc in each st to end of row, turn.
Rep last 2 rows 4 times more—18 sts.
**ROWS 11–14** Ch 2, hdc in each st to end of row, turn. Fasten off.
Rep for left sleeve.

## FINISHING
With RS tog, sew sleeve and side seams. With size D/3 (3.25mm) hook, attach A with a sl st to sleeve seam at lower edge. Work 1 row rev sc around each cuff edge. Fasten off.

## JACKET EDGING

Attach A with a sl st to right center front corner, ch 1, work 3 sc in each corner and sc in each st/row evenly around outer edge of jacket, having an even number of sts, join with a sl st to first sc.

**RND 1** With A, ch 2, **[with A, dc in next sc; with B, dc in same sc] into each corner st (6 sts each corner), *with A, dc in next sc; with B, dc in next sc; rep from * to next corner; rep from ** around, join with a sl st to first dc.

**RND 2** With B, ch 2, with appropriate color, BP tr around each of next 6 dc in corner, BP dc in each dc to next corner; rep from * around, join with a sl st to first st.

**RND 3** With B, ch 2, with appropriate color, BP dc in each st around, join with a sl st to first st. Break B.

**ROW 4** With A, ch 1, work rev sc in each st around, join with a sl st to first st. Fasten off. Sew separating zipper to center front edges, using photo as a guide.

## CAPRIS

### LEGS (MAKE 2)

With size D/3 (3.25mm) hook and A, ch 28.

**ROW 1** Hdc in 2nd ch from hook and in each ch across, turn—27 sts.

**ROWS 2–16** Ch 1, hdc in each hdc to end of row, turn. Do not cut A, attach B.

**ROWS 17 AND 18** With B, ch 1, hdc in each hdc to end of row, turn.

**ROWS 19 AND 20** With A, ch 1, hdc in each hdc to end of row, turn.

**ROWS 21 AND 22** With B, ch 1, hdc in each hdc to end of row, turn. Cut B.

**ROWS 23–38** With A, ch 1, hdc in each hdc to end of row, turn. Fasten off.

With WS tog, fold leg in half long sides tog, and sew 3"/7.5cm for leg inseam.

Place remainder of long edge of each leg tog and sew center front/back seam.

## WAISTBAND EDGING

With size D/3 (3.25mm) hook and RS facing, attach B with a sl st to top of center back seam.

**RND 1** Ch 1, work 38 sc evenly around top edge, join with a sl st to first sc.

**RND 2** Ch 3 (counts as 1 dc), dc in next sc and each sc around, join with a sl st to top of beg ch-3.

**RNDS 3 AND 4** Ch 1, sc in each dc around, join with a sl st to first sc. Fasten off.

## WAIST TIE

Make 12"/30.5cm chain. Weave ch through dc row on waist, starting and ending at center front.

## VISOR

### BAND

With size C/2 (2.75mm) hook and B, ch 61.

**ROW 1** Sc in 2nd ch from hook and each ch across, turn—60 sts.

**ROWS 2–4** Ch 1, sc in each sc to end of row, turn.

**ROW 5** Sl st in next 18 sts, sc in next 27 sts, sl st in next 15 sts. Fasten off.

### BILL

**ROW 6** With RS facing, B, and working on center 27 sc only, attach yarn with a sl st to first sc, ch 1, sc in same st as sl st, sc in next 26 sc, turn.

**ROW 7** Ch 1, sc2tog, sc in each st to last 2 sc, sc2tog, turn—25 sts. Rep last row until 7 sts rem. Fasten off.

With RS facing, attach A with a sl st to right edge at beg of visor bill. While holding flexible wire along visor edge, sc in each st/row and around wire to opposite edge of visor bill. Fasten off.

On WS where band and visor bill meet, work a row of sc on back side. Sew snap to each end of band to close. ✿

## Chart 1

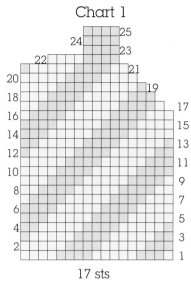

17 sts

## Chart 2

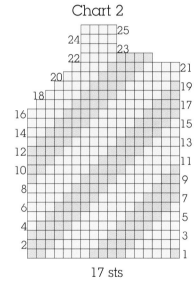

17 sts

## Color Key
- ▨ Gray (A)
- ☐ Yellow (B)

21

# Give It a Whirl

An airy dress with a pretty pinwheel on the bodice becomes an anytime ensemble with a matching jacket and purse.

## MATERIALS
- 2 1¾oz/50g balls (each approx 191yd/175m) of Red Heart *Stardust* (wool/nylon/metallic) in #B19 blue 🌀
- Size C/2 (2.75mm) hook OR SIZE TO OBTAIN GAUGE
- 3½"/1.5cm shell buttons (JHB #53179 used in sample)
- 16 glass E beads (6/0 Item BEA 4215 ¾ oz used in sample)

## GAUGE
20 sts and 16 rows = 4"/10cm over dc using size C/2 (2.75mm) hook. *Take time to check gauge.*

## STITCH GLOSSARY
**SCTBL** Single crochet in the back loop.
**DCTBL** Double crochet in the back loop.
**DCTFL** Double crochet in the front loop.

## NOTES
**1)** Dress top and skirt are worked separately, then sewn together.
**2)** Dress top is worked in one piece.

## DRESS
### CENTER MEDALLION
Ch 4, sl st to first ch to form ring.
**RND 1** Ch 5 (counts as 1 dc, ch 2), dc in ring, *ch 2, dc in ring; rep from * 6 times more, ch 2, join with sl st to 3rd ch of ch-5—8 dc and 8 ch-2 spaces.
**RND 2** Ch 1, sc in same st, 3 sc in 1st ch-2 sp, *sc in dc, 3 sc in next ch-2 sp; rep from * around, join with sl st to 1st sc—32 sts.
**RND 3** Ch 1, 3 sctbl in same st, sctbl in next 3 sc, *3 sctbl in next sc, sctbl in next 3 sc; rep from * around, join with sl st in 1st sc—48 sts.
**RND 4** Ch 1, sctbl in same st, *3 sctbl in next sc, sctbl in next 5 sc; rep from * around, end last rep sctbl in next 4 sc, join with sl st to 1st sc—64 sts.

**RND 5** Ch 1, sctbl in same sc, sctbl in next st, *3 sctbl in next sc, sctbl in next 7 sc; rep from * around, end last rep sctbl in next 5 sc, join with sl st to 1st sc—84 sts.
**RND 6** Ch 1, sctbl in same sc, sctbl in next 2 sc, *3 sctbl in next sc, sc in next 9 sc; rep from * around, end last rep sctbl in next 6 sc—96 sts. Do *not* join.
**RND 7** Ch 4, sk next 10 sc, *sc in next sc, bringing "point" to front of work, ch 4, sk next 11 sts; rep from * around, end last rep sk next 2 sts, join with a sl st to 1st ch of beg ch 4. Fasten off.

### FRONT TOP
Attach yarn with a sl st to any ch-4 sp of rnd 7 on medallion.
**RND 1** Ch 2, *3 dc in same ch-4 sp, [dc in next sc, 3 dc in next ch-4 sp] twice, dc in next sc, 2 dc in next ch-4 sp, [dc in next sc, 3 dc in next ch-4 sp] 3 times, dc in next sc, 2 dc in last ch-4 sp, dc in last sc, join with a sl st to 1st dc—30 dc.
**RND 2** Ch 3 (counts as 1 dc), dctbl in same st, 2 dctbl in each dc around, join with a sl st to 1st dc—60 dc.
**RND 3** Ch 3 (counts as 1 dc), dctbl in each dc around, join with a sl st to 1st dc.

**RND 4** Ch 3 (counts as 1 dc), [dctbl, ch 1, 2 dctbl] in same st, *dctbl in next 15 dc, [2 dctbl, ch 1, 2 dctbl] in next dc; rep from * twice more, dctbl in next 11 dc, join with a sl st to top of 1st dc.

### RIGHT SHOULDER AND BACK

**ROW 1** Sl st in next dc and ch-1 sp, ch 3 (counts as 1 dc), dctbl in next 4 dc, ch 12 (for right armhole), sk next 7 dc, dctbl in next 9 dc, 1 dc in ch-1 sp, turn.

**ROW 2** Ch 2, dctfl in first 10 dc, dc in each ch of 12-ch sp, dctfl in last 5 dc, turn—27 dc.

**ROW 3** Ch 2, dc2tog, dc in each dc to end of row, turn—26 dc.

**ROW 4** Ch 2, dctfl in each dc to last 2 dc, dc2tog tfl, turn—25 dc.

Rep last 2 rows twice more—21 dc. Fasten off.

### LEFT SHOULDER AND BACK

With RS facing, attach yarn to lower ch-1 sp of medallion.

**ROW 1** Ch 3 (counts as 1 dc), dctbl in next 9 dc, ch 12 (for left armhole), sk next 7 dc, dctbl in next 4 dc, dc in ch-1 sp, turn.

**ROW 2** Ch 2, dctfl in first 5 dc, dc in each ch of 12-ch sp, dctfl in last 10 dc, turn—27 dc.

**ROW 3** Ch 2, dc in each dc to last 2 dc, dc2tog, turn—26 dc.

**ROW 4** Ch 2, dc2tog tfl, dctfl in each dc to end of row, turn—25 dc.

Rep last 2 rows twice more—21 dc. Fasten off.

### SKIRT

Ch 95.

**ROW 1** Dc in 4th ch from hook (counts as 2 dc), dc in next 5 ch, *sk 2 ch, dc in next 5 ch, 3 dc in next ch, dc in next 5 ch; rep from * 5 times more, sk 2 ch, dc in next 5 ch, 2 dc in last ch, turn.

**ROW 2** Ch 3 (counts as 1 dc), dc in first dc, *dc in next 5 dc, sk 2 dc, dc in next 5 dc, 3 dc in next dc; rep from * 6 times more, ending last rep 2 dc in top of beg ch-3, turn.

Rep last row 8 times more.

**ROW 11** Ch 3 (counts as 1 dc), dc in first dc, *dc2tog, dc in next 3 dc, sk 2 dc, dc in next 3 dc, dc2tog, 3 dc in next dc; rep from * 6 times more, ending last rep 2 dc in top of beg ch-3, turn.

**ROW 12** Ch 3 (counts as 1 dc), dc in first dc, *dc2tog, dc in next 2 dc, sk 2 dc, dc in next 2 dc, dc2tog, 3 dc in next dc; rep from * 6 times more, ending last rep 2 dc in top of beg ch-3, turn.

**ROW 13** Ch 3 (counts as 1 dc), dc in each dc across.

**ROW 14** Ch 1, sc in each dc across. Fasten off.

### FINISHING

Sew center back seam of skirt. With front RS facing, match lower edge of dress top to top edge of skirt and sew in place, with last row of medallion circle overlapping in front. Sew buttons to RS of right back, placing the first at neck edge, the last ½"/1.5cm from dress top lower edge, and the remainder spaced evenly between (use spaces

between sts of left back as buttonholes). Sew 8 beads to row 2 of center medallion, using photo as a guide.

### PURSE

Work center medallion as given for dress. Attach yarn with a sl st to any ch-4 sp of rnd 7 on medallion.

**RND 1** Ch 3 (counts as 1 dc), 3 dc in same ch-4 sp, *dc in next sc, 4 dc in next ch-4 sp; rep from * 6 times more, dc in last sc, join with a sl st to top of ch-3—40 dc.

**RND 2** Ch 10, sk 10 dc, dc in each dc around, join with a sl st to first ch.

**RND 3** Ch 3 (counts as 1 dc), dc in next 9 ch, dc in dc around, join with a sl st to top of beg ch-3.

**RND 4** Ch 3 (counts as 1 dc), dc in each dc around, join with a sl st to top of beg ch-3.

**RND 5** *Dc2tog; rep from * around, join with a sl st to first dc—20 dc.

Rep last rnd twice more—5 dc. Cut yarn, pull through inside purse, and fasten off to close hole.

### HANDLE

Ch 35, sc in each ch to end of ch, turn.

**ROW 1** Sl st in each sc to end of row. Fasten off.

Sew each end of handle to purse opening. Sew 8 beads to row 2 of center medallion, using photo as a guide.

## JACKET

### RIGHT FRONT

Ch 15.

**ROW 1** 1 dc in 2nd ch from hook and in each ch to end of ch, turn—14 dc.

**ROW 2** Ch 3 (counts as 1 dc), sk first dc, *1 bpdc around next dc, 1 dc in next dc; rep from * to last dc, 1 bpdc around last dc, turn.

**ROW 3** Ch 2, 1 fpdc around first bpdc, dc in next dc, 1 fpdc around next bpdc, dc in next 2 sts, [2 dc in next st, dc in next st] 4 times, dc in last st, turn—18 dc.

**ROW 4** Ch 2, dc in first dc and next 14 dc, 1 bpdc around next fpdc, 1 dc in next dc, 1 bpdc around last fpdc; turn.

**ROW 5** Ch 2, 1 fpdc around first bpdc, 1dc in next dc, 1 fpdc around next bpdc, dc in each dc to end of row, turn.

Rep last 2 rows 4 times more. Fasten off.

### LEFT FRONT

Ch 15.

**ROW 1** 1 dc in 2nd ch from hook and in each ch to end of ch, turn—14 dc.

**ROW 2** Ch 3 (counts as 1 dc), sk first dc, *1 bpdc around next dc, 1 dc in next dc; rep from * to last dc, 1 bpdc in last dc, turn.

**ROW 3** Ch 2, dc in first dc, [dc in next st, 2 dc in next st] 4 times, dc in next 2 sts, 1 fpdc around next bpdc, dc in next dc, 1 fpdc around last bpdc, turn—18 dc.

**ROW 4** Ch 2, 1 bpdc around first fpdc, dc in next dc, 1 bpdc around next fpdc, dc in each st to end of row, turn.

**ROW 5** Ch 2, dc in each dc to last 3 sts, 1 fpdc around next bpdc, 1dc in next dc, 1 fpdc around last bpdc, turn.

Rep last 2 rows 4 times more. Fasten off.

### BACK

Ch 26.

**ROW 1** 1 dc in 2nd ch from hook and in each ch to end of ch, turn—25 dc.

**ROW 2** Ch 3 (counts as 1 dc), *1 bpdc around next dc, 1 dc in next dc; rep from * to end of row, turn.

**ROW 3** Ch 2, dc in first 2 dc, *2 dc in next st, dc in next st; rep from * to last st, dc in last st, turn—36 sts.

**ROW 4** Ch 2, dc in each dc to end of row, turn.

Rep last row 9 times more. Fasten off.

### SLEEVES

Ch 25.

**ROW 1** 1 dc in 2nd ch from hook and in each ch to end of ch, turn—24 dc.

**ROW 2** Ch 3 (counts as 1 dc), *1 bpdc around next dc, 1 dc in next dc; rep from * to last dc, 1 bpdc around last dc, turn.

**ROW 3** Ch 3 (counts as 1 dc), *1 dc in next dc, 1 fpdc around next bpdc; rep from * to end of row.

**ROW 4** Ch 2, dc in each dc to end of row, turn.

Rep last row 7 times more. Fasten off.

### FINISHING

Sew first and last 9 sts of back to right/left front for shoulder seams. Place markers 2½"/6.5cm down from each shoulder on side edge of front and back for armholes. Set in sleeves between markers. Sew side and sleeve seams.

### NECK EDGING

With RS facing, join yarn to right front neck edge.

**ROW 1** Ch 3 (counts as 1 dc), fpdc around next st, dc in next st, fpdc around next st, dc in each dc to last 4 sts, [fpdc around next st, dc in next st] twice, turn—25 sts.

**ROW 2** Ch 3 (counts as 1 dc), *bpdc around next st, dc in next st; rep from * to end of row.

**ROW 3** Ch 3 (counts as 1 dc), *fpdc around next st, dc in next st; rep from * to end of row. Fasten off. ✿

# Southern Belle

A vest constructed in a simple circle makes a bold but feminine statement worthy of Scarlett O'Hara.

## MATERIALS

- 1 1¾oz/50gr ball (each 136yd/125m) of Trendsetter Yarns *Merino VI* (superwash merino) in #2029 wine 3
- Size E/4 (3.5mm) hook OR SIZE TO OBTAIN GAUGE
- ⅜"/10mm-wide ribbon, 10"/25.5cm long

## GAUGE

24 sts and 12 rows = 4"/10cm over dc using size E/4 (3.5mm) hook. *Take time to check gauge.*

## STITCH GLOSSARY

**CROSS STITCH** Yo twice, insert hook in first dc, yo and draw through 2 loops on hook (3 loops remain on hook), yo, insert hook in next dc. Yo and draw through, yo and draw through 2 loops on hook 4 times, ch 2, yo, insert hook through middle of cross stitch and complete dc. The next cross stitch will begin in the same st where 2nd dc ended.

## VEST

Ch 6, join with a sl st to form ring.

**RND 1** Ch 3 (counts as 1 dc), work 17 dc in ring, join with sl st to top of beg ch-3—18 sts.

**RND 2** Ch 3 (counts as 1 dc), dc in next 2 dc, [ch 5, 1 dc in next 3 dc] 5 times, ch 5, join with a sl st to top of beg ch-3.

**RND 3** Ch 3 (counts as 1 dc), 1 dc in next 2 dc, [ch 5, sl st in next ch-5 sp, ch 5, dc in next 3 dc] 5 times, ch 5, sl st in next ch-5 sp, ch 5, join with a sl st to top of beg ch-3.

**RND 4** Ch 3 (counts as 1 dc), 1 dc in next 2 dc, [(ch 5, sl st in next ch-5 sp) twice, ch 5, 1 dc in next 3 dc] 5 times, [ch 5, sl st in next ch-5 sp] twice, ch 5, join with a sl st to top of beg ch-3.

**RND 5** Ch 3 (counts as 1 dc), 5 dc in next dc, 1 dc in next dc, sl st in next ch-5 sp, [ch 5, sl st in next ch-5 sp] twice, dc in next dc, [5 dc in next dc, dc in next dc] 5 times, [sl st in next ch-5 sp, ch 5] twice, join with a sl st to top of beg ch-3.

**RND 6** Ch 4 (counts as 1 dc, ch 1), 1 dc in next dc, [ch 1, dc in next dc] 5 times, *ch 10 (for armholes), sk next 2 ch-5 spaces, sl st in next dc, 1 dc in same dc, [ch 1, 1 dc in next dc] 6 times, **ch 5, sl st in next ch-5 sp, ch 5, dc in next dc, [ch 1, dc in next dc] 6 times, rep from * once more, then rep from ** once, ch 5, sl st in ch 5 space, ch 5, join with a sl st in 3rd ch of beg ch-4.

**RND 7** Ch 5 (counts as 1 dc, ch 2), 1 dc in next ch-1 sp, [ch 2, 1 dc in next ch-1 sp] 5 times, ch 5, sl st in ch-10 sp, ch 5, *1 dc in next dc, [ch 2, 1 dc in next ch-1 sp] 6 times, sl st in next ch-5 sp, ch 5, sl st in next ch-5 sp**, 1 dc in next dc, [ch 2, 1 dc in next ch-1 sp] 6 times, ch 5, sl st in ch-10 sp, ch 5; rep from * to ** 3 times more, join with a sl st in 3rd ch of beg ch-5.

**RND 8** Ch 4 (counts as 1 dc, ch 1), starting with first dc *[cross st

over next 2 dc] 6 times, *ch 4, sl st in next sl st, ch 4**, rep from * to * once more, sl st in next ch-5 sp, rep from * to ** once more, [(cross st over next 2 dc) 6 times, sl st in next ch-5 sp] 3 times, join with a sl st in 3rd ch of beg ch-4.

**RND 9** Ch 1, work 2 sc in each space around, working 5 sc in each ch-5 space—168 sts. Do not join.

**RND 10** Sl st in next 4 sc, ch 3 (counts as 1 dc), 1 dc in next 7 sc, ch 6, sk 6 sc, 1 dc in next 8 sc, ch 10, sk 8 sc, 1 dc in next 8 sc, ch 6, sk 6 sc, 1 dc in next 8 sc, ch 10, sk 4 sc, 1 dc in next 8 sc, ch 6, sk 6 sc, 1 dc in next 8 sc, ch 10, sk 8 sc, 1 dc in next 8 sc, ch 6, sk 6 sc, 1 dc in next 8 sc, ch 10, sk 4 sc, 1 dc in next 8 sc, ch 6, sk 6 sc, 1 dc in next 8 sc, ch 10, sk 4 sc, 1 dc in next 8 sc, ch 6, sk 6 sc, 1 dc in next 8 sc, ch 10, join with a sl st to top of beg ch-3.

**RND 11** *Ch 4, sk 4 dc, 1 sc in next dc, ch 4, sk next 4 dc, 10 dc in next ch-6 sp, ch 4, sk 4 dc, 1 sc in next dc, ch 4, 10 dc in next ch-10 sp; rep from * to end, join with a sl st to first ch in beg ch-4.

**RND 12** *Ch 4, 1 sc in next sc, ch 4, 1 dc in next 10 dc, rep from * to end, join with a sl st to first ch in beg ch-4. Fasten off.

**FINISHING**

ARMHOLE EDGINGS

With RS facing, attach yarn to armhole (rnd 6) and work 1 dc in each st/ch around opening, join with a sl st to first dc—22 sts. Fasten off. Thread ribbon through ch-4 sp to tie. ✿

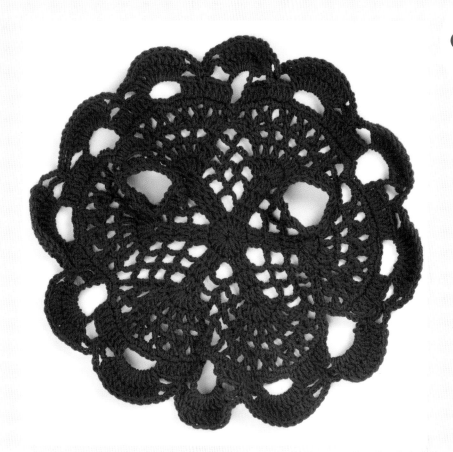

# Fit for a Fiesta

Add a little Latin flavor to her wardrobe with a layered chevron skirt and matching shawl. *Olé!*

## MATERIALS

- 1 .35oz/10g skein (each approx 49yd/45m) of DMC *Cotton Perlé 5* (cotton) each in #747 (A), #943 (B), #922 (C), #3753 (D), #368 (E), #754 (F), #578 (G), #524 (H), and #742 (I)
- Size C/2 (2.75mm) hook OR SIZE TO OBTAIN GAUGE
- Elastic thread
- 1"/2.5cm-wide ribbon, 20"/50.5cm long (optional)

## GAUGE

32 sts and 20 rows = 4"/10cm over chevron st using size C/2 (2.75mm) hook.
*Take time to check gauge.*

## STITCH GLOSSARY
**TFL (THROUGH FRONT LOOP)**
Work through front loop of st only.

## CHEVRON PATTERN

**ROW 1 (RS)** 2 sc in 2nd ch from hook, *sc in next 4 ch, sk 2 ch, sc in next 4 ch, 3 sc into next ch; rep from * across, ending last rep with 2 sc in last ch, turn.

**ROW 2** Ch 1, 2 sc in 1st st, *sc in next 4 sts, sk 2 sts, sc in next 4 sts, 3 sc into next st; rep from * across, ending last rep with 2 sc in last st, sk turning ch, turn.
Rep row 2 for chevron pat.

## SKIRT
### TOP
With A, ch 90.
**ROWS 1–18** Work chevron pat in each color thread in the following order, changing color of yarn every 2 rows: A, B, C, D, E, F, G, H, I. Cut yarn, attach G.
**ROW 19** Ch 2, hdc in first 2 sts, *dc in next 8 sts, hdc in next 3 sts; rep from * across, ending last rep with 1 hdc in last 2 sts.
Do *not* turn.
**ROWS 20 AND 22** Ch 1, rev sc in front lp only of each st across. Do *not* turn.
**ROW 21** Ch 2, dc in back lp of each st across. Do *not* turn.
**ROW 23** Ch 2, dc in next 18 sts, sl st in next 10 sts (underarm), dc in next 28 sts, sl st in next 10 sts, dc in next 18 sts. Do *not* turn.
**ROW 24** Ch 1, rev sc in each st across. Fasten off.

### LOWER EDGING
With RS facing, join A with a sl st to first foundation ch. Work 1 row rev sc along foundation ch to end of chain. Fasten off.

### BOTTOM
Work rows 1–18 as for skirt top with the foll color pat: A, B, C, F, E, D, G, H, I.

### LOWER EDGING
With RS facing, join A with a sl st to first foundation ch. Work 1 row rev sc along foundation ch to end of chain. Fasten off.

## FINISHING

Place skirt top over skirt bottom, thread tapestry needle with color B and sew tog, leaving A rows of top chevron pat loose for ruffle effect. Sew center back seam. Thread elastic thread through rev sc ridges of top and secure.

## SHAWL

With G, ch 55.

**ROW 1** Dc in 4th ch from hook, dc in each ch to end of ch, turn—52 sts.

**ROWS 2–4** Ch 2, dc tbl in each st across. Break G and join C.

**ROW 5** With C, ch 2, dc tbl in each st across.

**ROW 6** Ch 1, rev sc tfl in each st across. Break C and join F.

**ROW 7** With F, ch 2, dc tbl in each st across.

**ROW 8** Ch 1, rev sc tfl in each st across. Break F and join E.

**ROW 9** With E, ch 2, dc tbl in each st across.

**ROW 10** Ch 1, rev sc tfl in each st across. Break E and join D.

**ROW 11** With D, ch 2, dc tbl in each st across.

**ROW 12** Ch 1, rev sc tfl in each st across. Break D and join G.

**ROW 13** With G, ch 2, dc tbl in each st across. Fasten off.

## TIE EDGING

With RS facing, join F with a slip st to corner of one short side of shawl.

**ROW 1** Ch 2, work 16 dc evenly along short side edge, turn.

**ROW 2** Ch 2, skip first dc, 1 dc in each st across, turn—15 sts. Break F and join C.

**ROW 3** With C, ch 2, skip first dc, 1 dc in each st across, turn—14 sts.

**ROW 4** Ch 2, skip first dc, 1 dc in each st across, turn—13 sts. Break C and join D.

**ROW 5** With D, ch 2, skip first dc, 1 dc in each st across, turn—12 sts.

**ROW 6** Ch 2, skip first dc, 1 dc in each st across, turn—11 sts. Break D and join E.

**ROW 7** With E, ch 2, skip first dc, 1 dc in each st across, turn—10 sts.

With E, rep row 7 until 4 sts rem.

**NEXT ROW** Ch 2, 1 dc in each st across, join with a slip st to first dc to form a ring. Do not turn.

## I-CORD TIE

**NEXT RND** Work 1 sc in each st around, join with a sl st to first sc. Rep last rnd until I-cord tie measures 3"/7.5cm. Fasten off. Rep tie edging for rem short side of shawl. ✿

Use some brightly colored ribbon as a festive sash!

# A Night at the Opera

An ethereal lace shawl with a unique criss-cross construction adds extra glamour to a special evening frock.

## MATERIALS

- 1 1¾oz/50g ball (each approx 427yd/390m) of Debbie Bliss/KFI *Rialto Lace* (superwash merino) in #44011 blush (A) **[0]**
- 1 .88oz/25g ball (each approx 219yd/200m) of Debbie Bliss/KFI *Party Angel* (kid mohair/silk/metallic) in #15508 pink (B) **[0]**
- Size C/2 (2.75mm) hook OR SIZE TO OBTAIN GAUGE
- Stitch markers
- 2 snap fasteners
- 1 small gold button

## GAUGE

14 sts and 16 rows = 4"/10cm over main skirt pat using size C/2 (2.75mm) hook. *Take time to check gauge.*

## STITCH GLOSSARY

**FPDC (FRONT POST DC)** Yo, insert hook from front to back to front around post of designated st and draw up a lp, [yo and draw through 2 lps] twice.

**BPDC (BACK POST DC)** Yo, insert hook from back to front to back around post of designated st and draw up a lp, [yo and draw through 2 lps] twice.

## DRESS

### MAIN SKIRT

With B, ch 17.

**ROW 1** Sc in 2nd ch from hook and in each ch across, turn—17 sc.

**ROW 2** Ch 5 (counts as dc, ch 2), sk first 3 sc, dc in next sc, *ch 2, sk next 2 sc, dc in next sc; rep from * to end, turn.

**ROW 3** Ch 5 (counts as dc, ch 2), *dc in next dc, ch 2; rep from *, end dc in 3rd ch of beg ch-5, turn.

**ROW 4** Ch 1, sc in first dc, *2 sc in next ch-2 sp, sc in next dc; rep from *, end last rep sc in 3rd ch of beg ch-5, turn.

**ROW 5** Ch 1, sc in each sc across, turn.

Rep rows 2–5 another 13 times, then rows 2–4 once.

## TOP EDGING

Rotate to work along side length of piece.

**NEXT ROW** Ch 1, work 110 sc evenly along side edge of main skirt. Fasten off.

## SCALLOPED EDGE

With WS facing, attach yarn with a sl st to first sc on rem long side edge of main skirt.

**ROW 1** Ch 1, sc in same st as sl st, *ch 5, sc between ends of next 2 sc rows; rep from *, end sc in end of last sc row, turn.

**ROW 2** Ch 1, *[5 sc, ch 5, (3 sc, ch 5) twice, 5 sc] in ch-5 sp, sl st in next sc; rep from * to end. Fasten off. Sew short edges of main skirt together for center back seam. Sew ends of scalloped edge together.

## LOWER RUFFLE

With B, ch 122.

**ROW 1** Sc in 2nd ch from hook and each ch across, turn—121 sc.

**ROW 2** Ch 5 (counts as dc, ch 2), sk first 3 sc, dc in next sc, *ch 2, sk next 2 sc, dc in next sc; rep from * to end, turn.

## SKIRT

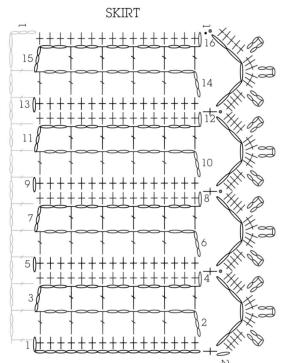

## Stitch Key

- • slip stitch (sl st)
- ⌒ chain (ch)
- ✛ single crochet (sc)
- ⊤ double crochet (dc)
- 〇 draw up a loop

## ASSEMBLY DIAGRAM

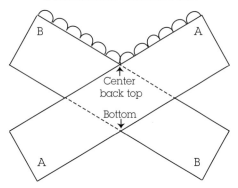

**ROW 3** Ch 5 (counts as dc, ch 2), *dc in next dc, ch 2; rep from *, end dc in 3rd ch of beg ch-5, turn.

**ROW 4** Ch 1, sc in first dc, *2 sc in next ch-2 sp, sc in next dc; rep from *, end last rep sc in 3rd ch of beg ch-5, turn.

**ROW 5** Ch 1, sc in each sc across, turn.

Rep rows 2–5 once more. Fasten off. Sew short side edges together for center back seam. Place last row of lower ruffle behind scallop edging and sew to main skirt, leaving scallop edging free.

### UPPER RUFFLE

With B, ch 122. Work rows 1–4 as given for lower ruffle.

**ROW 5** Ch 5 (counts as dc, ch 2), sk first 3 sc, dc in next sc, *ch 2, sk next 2 sc, dc in next sc; rep from * to end, turn.

**ROW 6** Ch 1, sc in first dc, *ch 5, sk next dc, sc in next dc; rep from * to end of row. Fasten off. Sew short side edges together for center back seam.

### TOP

With RS facing and A, attach yarn with a sl st to 1st sc at center back of top edge of skirt.

**RND 1** Ch 3 (counts as dc), sk first sc, dc in each sc across, join with a sl st to first sc—110 dc. Place marker for beg of rnd.

**RND 2** *FPdc around next dc, BPdc around next dc; rep from * around.

**RNDS 3 AND 4** *FPdc around next FPdc, BPdc around next BPdc around.

**RND 5** FPdc around 1st FPdc, *sk next BPdc, FPdc around next FPdc; rep from * around—55 FPdc.

Rep last rnd 15 times more.

**RND 21** FPdc around each FPdc to last 18 sts, sl st across last 18 sts for left back, then across first 17 sts of next rnd for right back.

**ROW 22** FPdc around next 20 sts for front, turn.

**ROW 23** Ch 2, working on rem 20 front sts, BPdc around each st to end of row, turn.

**ROW 24** Ch 2, FPdc around first 6 BPdc, turn. Work BPdc and FPdc alternately on these 6 sts for 15 rows. Fasten off.

With RS facing, sk next 8 FPdc for center front. Attach yarn and FPdc around last 6 FPdc, turn. Work BPdc and FPdc alternately on these 6 sts for 15 rows. Fasten off.

### FINISHING

Place first row of upper ruffle over joining row of top and main skirt, matching center back seams. Sew upper ruffle to main skirt. Sew snap fasteners to ends of top straps.

### HONEYCOMB SHAWL (MAKE 2)

With B, ch 32.

**ROW 1** Dc in 8th ch from hook (counts as 1 dc, ch 3, 1 dc), *ch 3, sk 3 ch, dc in next ch; rep from * to end, turn—8 dc and 7 ch-3 sps.

**ROW 2** Ch 6 (counts as 1 dc, ch 3), BPdc around 2nd dc, *ch 3, BPdc around next dc; rep from * to end of row, turn.

Rep row 2 until piece measures 12"/30.5cm. Do not fasten off. Turn work 90 degrees clockwise.

### EDGING

Working down long left side, work 1 sc in each end-of-row st and each ch-3 sp for approx 5". Fasten off. Rep on other shawl piece, on long right side (see diagram).

### FLOWER

Ch 2.

**RND 1** 6 sc in 2nd ch from hook. Join with sl st to first sc.

**RND 2** Ch 1, 2 sc in each sc around—12 sc. Join with sl st to first sc.

**RND 3** Ch 1, 2 sc in each sc around—24 sc. Join with sl st to first sc.

**RND 4** Working in front loops *only*, *[ch 3, 1 tr] in same sc, [2 tr in next sc] twice, 1 tr in next sc, ch 3, sl st in same sc, sl st in next sc; rep from * around. Join with sl st in base of beg ch. Fasten off.

Attach gold button in center of crocheted flower.

## FINISHING

**NOTE** The long side with edging is the neck edge.

Lay one piece flat on top of the other, neck edge at top/away from you and short sides to right and left. The piece on top is A, the piece on bottom is B. Following diagram, tack the two pieces tog at the center of neck edge. Sew the right-hand short-side edges together. On left-hand side, bring piece B to top of A without twisting and sew the left-hand short-sides tog. Tack pieces A and B at lower edge, opposite neck tack. Attach snap at neck edge of each seam. Sew flower over top half of snap.

## COLLAR

With RS facing, attach B to start of neck edge at snap fastener.

**ROW 1** Ch 2, dc in each sc across, turn.

**ROW 2** *Ch 6, skip next 2 dc, tr in next dc; rep from * to end, turn.

**ROW 3** [Ch 5, 2 sc, ch 5, 2 sc, ch 5, 2 sc] in each ch-6 sp across. Fasten off. ✿

# Hip to Be Square

Get into a '70s groove with a granny square top, bell sleeves, a bandana, and a fabric maxi skirt.

## MATERIALS

- 1 .35oz/10g ball (each approx 49yd/45m) of DMC *Coton Perlé 5* each in #3053 green (B), and #740 orange (C)
- 2 balls each in #597 blue (A) and #712 cream (D)
- Size B/1 (2.25mm) hook OR SIZE TO OBTAIN GAUGE
- 2 small snaps
- Fabric 13"/33cm long x 21"/53.5cm wide
- Stitch markers
- 1 bead (for bandana flower center)

## GAUGES

24 dc and 12 rows = 4"/10cm over dc using size B/1 (2.25mm) hook.
One square = 2½"/6.5cm using size B/1 (2.25mm) hook.
*Take time to check gauges.*

## TOP

### FRONT MOTIF

With D, ch 6. Join with a sl st in first ch to form a ring.

**RND 1** Ch 6 (counts as 1 dc, ch 3), *dc in ring, ch 3; rep from * 6 more times, join with sl st to 3rd ch. Fasten off.

**RND 2** Join A to any ch-3 sp, ch 3 (counts as 1 dc), 3 dc in same sp, *ch 2, 4 dc in next ch-3 sp; rep from * 6 more times, ch 2, join with sl st to top of beg ch-3. Fasten off.

**RND 3** Join B to any ch-2 sp, ch 3 (counts as 1 dc), 5 dc in same sp, *ch 1, 6 dc in next ch-2 sp, ch 3, 6 dc in next ch-2 sp; rep from * twice more, ch 1, 6 dc in next ch-2 sp, ch 3, join with sl st to top of beg ch-3. Fasten off.

**RND 4** Join C to any ch-1 sp, sc in same ch-1 sp, *ch 3, sc between 3rd and 4th dc of next 6dc group, ch 3, (2 dc, 3 ch, 2 dc) into ch-3 space, ch 3, sc between 3rd and 4th dc of next 6dc grp, ch 3, sc into ch-1 sp; rep from * twice more, ch 3, sc between 3rd and 4th dc of next 6dc group, ch 3, [2 dc, 3 ch, 2 dc] into ch-3 space, ch 3, sc between 3rd and 4th dc of next 6dc grp, join with sl st to first sc. Fasten off.

**RND 5** Join D with a sl st to back loop of any 2nd ch of ch-3 sp, [sctbl, ch 1, sctbl] in same st,

*skip next ch, sctbl in next 2 sts, [sctbl in next ch, skip next ch, sctbl in next ch, sctbl in next st] 4 times, sctbl in next st, skip next ch, [sctbl, ch 1, sctbl] in next ch; rep from * twice more, skip next ch, sctbl in next 2 sts, [sctbl in next ch, skip next ch, sctbl in next ch, sctbl in next st] 4 times, sctbl of next st, skip next ch, join with a sl st tbl of first sc.

**RND 6** Sl st in first sc and ch-1 sp, ch 3 (counts as 1 dc), 2 dc in same ch-1 sp, *skip next dc, dc in each of next 15 sts, skip next dc, 3 dc in ch-1 sp; rep from * twice more, skip next st, dc in each of next 15 sts, skip next st, join with a sl st to top of beg ch-3.

### LEFT ARMHOLE/LEFT BACK

**ROW 1** Skip first dc, sl st in next dc, ch 3 (counts as 1 dc), 2 dc in same dc as sl st, [ch 1, skip next dc, 3 dc in next dc] 3 times, ch 20, skip next 11 sts (left armhole), 2 dc in next dc, turn, leaving rem sts unworked.

**ROW 2** Ch 3, skip first dc, dc in next dc, skip first ch, dc in each of next 19 ch, ch 1, [3 dc in each ch-1 sp, ch 1] 3 times, dc in top of beg ch-3, turn.

**ROW 3** Skip first dc, sl st in ch-1 sp, ch 3 (counts as 1 dc), 2 dc in same ch-1 sp, [ch 1, 3 dc in next ch-1 sp] 3 times, dc in each dc to last st, skip beg ch-3. Fasten off.

**ROW 4** With RS facing, attach C with a sl st to top of beg ch-3. Ch 3 (counts as 1 dc), [skip next dc, dc in each of next 2 dc] 3 times, dc in each dc to end—29 dc. Fasten off.

**ROW 5** With RS facing, attach B, with a sl st to top of beg ch-3. Ch 3 (counts as 1 dc), 2 dc in same st, *ch 1, skip 2 dc, 3 dc in next dc; rep from * to last st, dc in last dc. Fasten off.

**ROW 6** With RS facing, attach A with a sl st to top of beg ch-3. Ch 3, *3 dc in next ch-1 sp, ch 1; rep from * to last 3 sts, dc in last st, turn. Fasten off.

**ROW 7** With RS facing, attach D with a sl st to top of beg ch-3. Ch 3, *3 dc in next ch-1 sp, ch 1; rep from * to last 3 sts, dc in last st, turn. Fasten off.

### RIGHT ARMHOLE/RIGHT BACK

With RS facing, attach D with a sl st in the center dc of upper right 3dc corner of front motif.

**ROW 1** Ch 3, dc in same st, ch 20, skip next 11 dc, [3 dc in next dc, skip next st, ch 1] 3 times, skip next st, 3 dc in next dc, turn.

**ROW 2** Ch 4 (counts as 1 dc, ch 1), [3 dc in next ch-1 sp, ch 1] 3 times, dc in each of next 19 ch, skip last ch, dc in next dc, turn.

**ROW 3** Ch 3 (counts as 1 dc), skip first dc, dc in each of next 19 dc, [3 dc in next ch-1 sp, ch 1] 3 times, 3 dc in last ch-1 sp. Fasten off.

**ROW 4** With WS facing, attach C with a sl st to top of beg ch-3. Ch 3 (counts as 1 dc), [skip next dc, dc in each of next 2 dc] 3 times, dc in each dc to end—29 dc. Fasten off.

**ROW 5** With WS facing, attach B, with a sl st to top of beg ch-3. Ch 3 (counts as 1 dc), 2 dc in same st, *ch 1, skip 2 dc, 3 dc in next dc; rep from * to last st, dc in last dc. Fasten off.

**ROW 6** With WS facing, attach A with a sl st to top of beg ch-3. Ch 3, *3 dc in next ch-1 sp, ch 1; rep from * to last 3 sts, dc in last st, turn. Fasten off.

**ROW 7** With WS facing, attach D with a sl st to top of beg ch-3. Ch 3, *3 dc in next ch-1 sp, ch 1; rep from * to last 3 sts, dc in last st, turn. Fasten off.

### TOP EDGING

With RS facing, attach C with a sl st to upper right back edge, sc in each st to last st, 3 sc in last st, work 41 sc evenly along bottom edge to lower left back corner, 3 sc in next st, sc in each st to neck edge. Fasten off.

### HEM EDGING

With RS facing, attach A with a sl st to center st of right back hemline corner.

**ROW 1** Ch 3 (counts as 1 dc), skip corner sc, dc in each of next 5 sc, [skip next sc, ch 3, dc in each of next 6 dc] 5 times, turn.

**ROW 2** Ch 3, [7 tr in next ch-3 sp, ch 2, sc between next 3rd and 4th dc, ch 2] 5 times, join with a sl st to last dc. Fasten off.

### NECK EDGE

With RS facing, attach B with a sl st to base of last edging sc at left back neck edge.

**ROW 1** Work 1 sc around side edge of next row, 2 sc around side edge each of next 2 rows, [6 dc around side edge of next row, 1 sc around side edge of next row] 3 times, sc in next 17 sts along top of front motif, [1 sc around side edge of next row, 6 dc around side edge of next row] 3 times, 2 sc around side edge each of next 2 rows, 1 sc around side edge of last row. Fasten off.

Sew snap to neck edges, placing left back over right back.

## BELL SLEEVE (MAKE 2)

With RS facing, attach A with a sl st to center st of underarm.

**RND 1** Ch 2, work 33 dc evenly around armhole opening, join with a sl st to first dc.

**RND 2** Ch 2, 1 dc in each of next 15 dc, dc3tog, 1 dc in each of next 15 dc, join with a sl st to first dc—31 sts.

**RND 3** Ch 2, 1 dc in each of next 14 dc, dc3tog, 1 dc in each of next 12 dc, dc2tog, join with a sl st to first dc—28 sts.

**RND 4** Ch 2, dc2tog, 1 dc in each of next 11 dc, dc3tog, 1 dc in each of next 12 dc, join with a sl st to first dc—25 sts.

**RND 5** Ch 2, 1 dc in each of next 11 dc, dc3tog, 1 dc in each of next 9 dc, dc2tog, join with a sl st to first dc—22 sts.

**RND 6** Ch 2, dc2tog, 1 dc in each of next 8 dc, dc3tog, 1 dc in each of next 9 dc, join with a sl st to first dc—19 sts.

**RNDS 7 AND 8** Ch 2, 1 dc in each of st around, join with a sl st to first dc.

**RND 9** Ch 2, 2 dc in each st around, join with a sl st to first dc—38 sts.

**RNDS 10 AND 11** Ch 2, 1 dc in each st around. Fasten off.

## BANDANA

With D, ch 51.

**ROW 1** Dc in 4th ch from hook and each ch across, turn—48 sts.

**ROW 2** Ch 6 (counts as 1 dc, ch 3), *skip next 3 sts, dc in next st, ch 3; rep from * to last ch, dc in last ch, turn—13 dc, 12 ch-3 sps.

**ROW 3** Ch 6 (counts as 1 dc, ch3), skip first dc, *dc in next dc, ch 3; rep from * to last st, dc in 3rd ch of ch-6, turn. Break D and join C.

**ROWS 4 AND 5** With C, rep row 3. Break C and join A.

**ROW 6** With A, ch 2, skip first dc, *dc in next dc, ch 3; rep from * to last st, dc in 3rd ch of beg ch-6, turn.

**ROW 7** With A, ch 2, skip first dc, *dc in next dc, ch 3; rep from * to last st, dc in last dc, turn—11 dc, 10 ch-3 sps. Break A and join B.

**ROWS 8 AND 9** With B, rep row 3. Break B and join D.

**ROWS 10 AND 11** With D, rep rows 6 and 7—9 dc, 8 ch-3 sps.

**ROWS 12 AND 13** With D, rep row 6. Break D and join B.

**ROW 14** With B, rep row 6. Break B and join A.

**ROW 15** With A, rep row 6. Break A and join C.

**ROWS 16, 17, 18, 20, AND 22** With C, rep row 6.

**ROWS 19, 21, AND 23** With C, rep row 7—3 dc, 2 ch-3 sps. Fasten off.

### FINISHING

**EDGING**

With RS facing, attach D to first dc of row 1.

**ROW 1** Work 1 row sc evenly around bandana to opposite dc of row 1, having a multiple of 3 sts plus 1 st, turn.

**ROW 2** Ch 1, sc in first sc, *ch 3, skip next 2 sts, sc in next st; rep from * around, ch 50 (for first tie), turn.

**ROW 3** Dc in 3rd ch from hook and in next 47 ch, *[sc, 4 dc, sc] in each ch-3 sp; rep from * around, ch 50, turn, dc in 3rd ch from hook and in next 47 ch, join to first sc with a sl st. Fasten off.

## FLOWER

With D, ch 3.

**RND 1** [4 dc, ch 3] 4 times in 1st ch, join with a sl st to first dc. Fasten off.

**RND 2** Attach A with a sl st in center of any 4 dc, ch 1, sc in same st, *ch 4, skip 2 dc and ch-3 sp, dc in next dc, ch 4, skip next 3 dc and ch-3 sp, sc in next dc; rep from * around, join with a sl st to first sc. Fasten off.

Sew bead to center of flower. Sew flower to bandana, using photo as a placement guide.

## SKIRT

Fold lower edge of fabric over ¼"/0.5cm, then ¾"/2cm again to hem. With sewing machine, stitch the hem ⅝" from lower edge. Press.

Fold top edge of fabric over ¼"/0.5cm, then ½"/1.5cm again to hem. With sewing machine, make 2 rows of running stitches through hem. Sew center back seam of skirt, leaving 2½"/6.5cm opening at upper edge.

Baste 2 rows of gathering stitches along top of skirt. Pull gathering threads to fit waist and secure. Sew snaps to back opening at upper edge. ✿

# Daisy Mays

Freshen up the dollhouse with a bouquet
of colorful crocheted daisies.

## MATERIALS

- 1 1¾oz/50g hank (each approx 108yd/97m) of Tahki▪Stacy Charles, Inc. *Cotton Classic* (mercerized cotton) in #3533 bright yellow (A), #3001 white (B), #3488 dark red (C), #3725 deep leaf green (D), and #3214 coffee (E)
- Size F/5 (3.75mm) hook OR SIZE TO OBTAIN GAUGE

## NOTE

Use color D for the leaves; color E for the centers, and color A, B, or C for the petals.

## FLOWER

### PETALS

Ch 10. Join with sl st in first ch to form a ring.

**RND 1** Ch 1, 24 sc in ring. Join with sl st to first sc.

**RND 2** *Ch 14, 1 sc in 2nd ch from hook and in each ch to end (petal made), 1 sc in next 2 sc of ring; rep from * around—12 petals. Join with sl st to first ch of beg ch—14.

**RND 3** *1 sc in each foundation ch along side of next petal to last ch, 5 sc in last ch (working around to other side of petal), 1 sc in each sc along side of petal, skip next sc of ring, 1 sc in next sc; rep from * for each petal. Join with sl st to first sc.
Fasten off.

### CENTER

Ch 2.

**RND 1** 5 sc in 2nd ch from hook.

**RND 2** Working in a spiral in back lps only, 2 sc in each st to end—10 sc.

**RND 3** *1 sc in next st, 2 sc in next st; rep from * to end—15 sc. Rep rnd 3, end 1 sc in last st—22 sc. Join with sl st to first sc. Fasten off, leaving a long tail. Stuff center with scrap yarn, then thread tail through top edge of last rnd and pull tightly to gather. Fasten securely. Sew to center of flower.

### LEAVES

Ch 10. Join with sl st in first ch to form a ring.

**RND 1** Ch 1, 24 sc in ring. Join with sl st to first sc.

**RND 2** Ch 15, 1 sc in 2nd ch from hook, 1 hdc in next ch, 1 dc in next ch, 1 tr in next 8 ch, 1 dc in next ch, 1 hdc in next ch, 1 sc in next ch (leaf made), sl st in next sc of ring. Turn.

**ROW 3** Ch 1, 1 sc in each st along side of leaf, 3 sc in end ch of last st (working around to other side of petal), 1 sc in each foundation ch along side of leaf, sl st in next sc of ring. Turn.

**ROW 4** Working in back lps only across RH side of leaf, ch 1, 1 sc in each st along side of leaf to center of 3-sc group, 3 sc in center st, 1 sc in each st along side of leaf, sl st in next sc of ring. For second leaf, 1 sc in next 2 sc of ring and rep rows 1–4. Fasten off.

## FINISHING

Position leaves behind flower as desired and sew in place. ✿

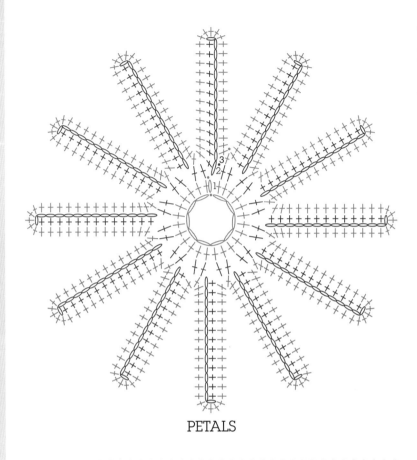

**PETALS**

**CENTER**

## Stitch Key

- slip stitch (sl st)
- chain (ch)
- single crochet (sc)
- double crochet (dc)
- treble crochet (tr)
- draw up a loop

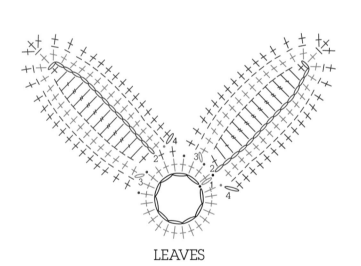

**LEAVES**

# Wildflower

This hat, scarf, and mitten set composed of colorful petals looks like it was picked from a flowerbed.

## MATERIALS

- 2 1¾oz/50g balls (each approx 175yd/160m) of Koigu *KPPPM* (merino) in #3611 ②
- Size C/2 (2.75mm) hook OR SIZE TO OBTAIN GAUGE
- Tapestry needle

## GAUGE

3 scallops and 5 rows = 3"/7.5cm using size C/2 (2.75mm) hook. *Take time to check gauge.*

## CROCODILE PATTERN

**ROW 1 (WS)** Dc in 3rd ch from hook (counts as 2 dc), *ch 2, sk 2 ch, 1 dc in next ch, ch 2, sk 2 ch, 2 dc in next ch; rep from * to end of ch, turn work 90 degrees clockwise.

**ROW 2** Ch 1, *working from top to bottom, work 5 dc around post of next dc, ch 1, turn work 180 degrees clockwise and, working from bottom to top, work 5 dc around post of next dc, ch 1, turn work to WS and sl st in next dc, turn work to RS, ch 1; rep from * to last 2 dc, working from top to bottom, work 5 dc around post of next dc—1 crocodile st made, ch 1, turn work 90 degrees clockwise and working from bottom to top, work 5 dc around post of next dc, turn work 90 degrees clockwise.

**ROW 3** Ch 1, 1 dc in center of next crocodile st, ch 2, *[1 dc in next ch-2 sp from row 1] twice, ch 2, 2 dc in center of next crocodile st, ch 2; rep from * to last end of row, ending with ch 1 and turning work 90 degrees clockwise.

**ROW 4** Ch 1, *working from top to bottom, work 5 dc around post of next dc, ch 1, turn work 180 degrees clockwise and, working

from bottom to top, work 5 dc around post of next dc, ch 1, turn work to WS and sl st in next dc, turn work to RS, ch 1; rep from * to last dc, sl st in last dc, turn work to RS.

**ROW 5** Ch 3 (counts as 1 dc), 1 dc into first sl st, *ch 2, 1 dc in center of next crocodile st, ch 2, [1 dc in next ch-2 sp from row 3]

twice; rep from * to last ch-2 sp from row 3, 2 dc in last ch-2 sp, turn work 90 degrees clockwise. Rep rows 2–5 for crocodile pat.

## SCARF (MAKE 2)
### RIGHT HALF
Ch 21.
Work 15 rows in crocodile pat, end with row 3.
**ROW 16** Ch 21 (this will make the slot for holding left side of scarf), sk to last st of previous row and sl st to last dc.
**ROWS 17–37** Starting with row 1, work a further 21 rows in crocodile pat, end with row 5. Fasten off.

### LEFT HALF
Ch 21. Work in crocodile pat for 37 rows, ending with row 5. Fasten off.
Sew right side and left side together at neck edge. For wearing, lace left side through slot in right side.

## MITTENS (MAKE 2)
### CUFF
Ch 8.
**ROW 1** Hdc in 2nd ch from hook and next 6 ch, turn—7 sts.
**ROW 2** Ch 2, dc in front lower lp of next 7 hdc, turn.
**ROW 3** Ch 2, hdc in front loop of next 7 dc, turn.
Rep rows 2 and 3 eight more times. Do not cut yarn. Join cuff in the rnd by folding in half and sl st to close, ch 2.

### HAND
**RND 1 (RS)** Work 21 hdc evenly around cuff—21 sts.
**RND 2** Hdc in each st around.
**RND 3** Hdc in next 4 hdc (thumb), hdc in next 17 hdc, leave last 4 hdc of rnd unworked.
**RND 4** Sk 4 unworked hdc and 1st 4 hdc for thumb, hdc in next 17 hdc (leaving 8 thumb sts open), AT THE SAME TIME, inc 1 hdc every 2nd stitch around—25 sts.
**RND 5** Hdc in each st around.
**RNDS 6 AND 7** Hdc in first st, [hdc2tog] 12 times—13 sts.
**RND 8** Sl st rem sts and pull tight to close. Fasten off.
Turn mittens to WS and stitch thumb opening tog to close.

## HAT
Ch 60.
Work rows 1–5 of crocodile pat.
**ROW 4** Sl st to join in rnd, work 72 dc evenly around, join with a sl st to first dc—72 dc.
**ROW 5** Ch 3 (counts as 1 dc), dc in each st around, join with a sl st to first dc.
**ROW 6** *Dc2tog; rep from * to end of rnd—36 sts.
**RNDS 7 AND 8** *Dc2tog; rep from * to end of rnd—9 sts.
**RND 9** [Dc2tog] 4 times, dc in last st – 5 sts. Fasten off.
Sl st top closed. Sew 4 open rows at lower edge together for center back seam.

## TOP EMBELLISHMENT
Ch 15.
Work rows 1 and 2 of crocodile pat—3 scallops made. Fasten off.
Sew ends of beg ch together to form a ring and sew to top of hat. ✿

## CROCODILE STITCH

### Even Rows

### Odd Rows

## Stitch Key

- • slip stitch (sl st)
- ⌒ chain (ch)
- ⊤ double crochet (dc)

# Slip into Sleepytime

A robe of super-soft chenille is cozy as can be,
especially when paired with cute kitten slippers!

## MATERIALS

- 3 1¾oz/50g balls (each approx 74yd/68m) of Plymouth Yarn *Adore* (nylon) in #5 yellow (A) ⑥
- 1 ball in #1 white (B)
- Small amount pink and blue embroidery thread (for slippers)
- Size G/6 (4mm) hook OR SIZE TO OBTAIN GAUGE
- Stitch markers

## GAUGE

13 sts and 8 rows = 4"/10cm over dc using size G/6 (4mm) hook. *Take time to check gauge.*

## NOTES

1) Body of robe is worked in one piece, starting at right side edge and working to left side edge.
2) Sleeves are worked from top down after sewing side seams.

## ROBE

### RIGHT FRONT AND BACK

With A, ch 81.

**ROW 1 (RS)** Dc in 2nd ch from hook and each ch to end of row, turn—80 sts.

**ROWS 2–4** Dc in each dc across, turn.

**ROW 5 (WS)** Dc in next 40 dc, place marker #1 for right shoulder, dc in next 22 dc, place marker #2 for start of collar, dc to end of row. Cut yarn.

**ROW 6 (RS)** With RS facing, attach yarn at marker #1. Dc in each dc to end of row, turn—40 sts. Working on these 40 sts only, work a further 6 rows, end with a RS row.

**ROW 13 (WS)** Dc in next 40 dc, ch 41, turn.

### LEFT FRONT AND BACK

**ROW 14** Dc in 2nd ch from hook, dc in next 17 ch, place marker #3 for end of collar, dc in next 22 ch, place marker #4 for left shoulder, and dc in each dc to end, turn—80 sts.

**ROWS 15–19** Dc in each dc across, turn. Cut yarn.

**ROW 20** With RS facing, attach B at marker #2. Work 1 tr in each dc to marker #1, 2 tr in each row to marker #4, 1 tr in each dc to marker #3, ch 3, turn.

**ROW 21** Tr in each tr. Fasten off. Fold fronts and back together, matching lower edge of back with lower edge of fronts. Starting at lower edge, sew side seams, leaving last 4"/10cm open on each side for armholes.

## SLEEVES (MAKE 2)

With RS facing, attach A to underarm seam, ch 2 (counts as 1 dc), work 23 dc evenly around armhole opening, join with a sl st in top of beg ch-2—24 sts.

**RND 1** Ch 2 (counts as 1 dc), dc2tog, dc in each dc to last 2 dc, dc2tog—22 sts.

Rep rnd 1 until 18 sts rem. Fasten off.

## FINISHING

With B, embroider scroll along bottom edge of robe front in running stitch, using photo as a guide.

## BELT

With B, ch 90.

**ROW 1** Dc in 2nd ch from hook, dc in each ch across. Fasten off.

## SLIPPERS (MAKE 2)

With A, ch 10.

**ROW 1** Sc in each ch, turn.

**ROW 2** Sc in next 5 sc, sl st in each next 4 sc, ch 1, turn.

**ROW 3** Sl st next 4 sl st, sc in next 5 sc, ch 1, turn.

**ROW 4** Sc in next 5 sc, sl st in next 4 sl st.

**ROW 5** Rep row 3.

**ROW 6** Ch 1, dc in each st across toe area, ch 2, turn—8 sts.

**ROW 7** 2 dc in 1st dc, dc in each dc, 2 dc in last dc, ch 2, turn—10 sts.

**ROW 8** [Dec 1 dc, dc, dec 1] across, ch 2, turn.

## EARS

**ROW 9** Dc in next st, sl st down dc just made, sl st in next 3 sts, dc in next st, ch 2, sl st in last st.

**ROW 10** Sl st in each st around slipper to left ear. Embroider white stripes across (see photo).

## FINISHING

With WS together, fold slipper upper approx 1"/2.5cm over sole area, with side edges meeting. Sew side edges. Embroider cat face and whiskers, using photo as a guide. ✿

Personalize your kittens with different colors of embroidery thread!

# Circus of Color

Bright stripes, a rainbow of buttons down the front, and a flowered bag make this dress a fun showstopper.

## MATERIALS

- 1 10g sampler pack of Presencia *Finca Perlé Cotton 3* (cotton) in #816/03S jewel: #159 gold (A), #263 red (B), #773 purple (C), #140 blue (D), #295 green (E), and #375 pumpkin (F) **10**
- Size C/2 (2.75mm) hook OR SIZE TO OBTAIN GAUGE
- 2 snaps
- One package (12) miniature doll buttons (optional)

## GAUGE

26 sts and 8 rows = 4"/10cm over tr and dc using size C/2 (2.75mm) hook. *Take time to check gauge.*

## NOTES

**1)** Dress is worked horizontally in one piece, starting at center front and ending at center back.
**2)** Collar is worked separately and sewn in position.

## DRESS

### RIGHT FRONT

With A, ch 49.

**ROW 1 (WS)** Sc in 2nd ch from hook, sc in next 11 ch, hdc in next 12 ch, dc in next 12 ch, tr in next 12 ch, turn—48 sts.

**ROW 2** Ch 4 (counts as 1 tr), skip first st, tr in next 11 sts, dc in next 12 sts, hdc in next 12 sts, sc in last 12 sts. Break A and join C.

**ROW 3** With C, ch 1, sc in first 12 sts, hdc in next 12 sts, dc in next 12 sts, tr in next 12 sts, turn.

**ROW 4** Ch 4 (counts as 1 tr), skip first st, tr in next 11 sts, dc in next 12 sts, hdc in next 12 sts, sc in last 12 sts. Break C and join F.

**ROWS 5 AND 6** With F, work rows 3 and 4. Break F and join E.

**ROWS 7 AND 8** With E, work rows 3 and 4. Break E and join D.

**ROWS 9 AND 10** With D, work rows 3 and 4. Break D and join A.

Row 11 With A, work row 3.

### RIGHT ARMHOLE OPENING/RIGHT BACK

**ROW 12** Ch 4 (counts as 1 tr), skip first st, tr in next 11 sts, dc in next 12 sts, hdc in next 12 sts, turn, leaving rem sts unworked. Break A and join B.

**ROW 13** With B, ch 1, hdc in next 12 sts, dc in next 12 sts, tr in next 12 sts, turn.

**ROW 14** Ch 4 (counts as 1 tr), skip first st, tr in next 11 sts, dc in next 12 sts, hdc in next 12 sts. Break B and join C.

**ROWS 15 AND 16** With C, work rows 13 and 14. Break C and join F.

**ROWS 17 AND 18** With F, work rows 13 and 14. Break F and join D.

**ROWS 19 AND 20** With D, work rows 13 and 14. Fasten off.

### LEFT FRONT

With RS facing, attach B with a sl st to 1st sc of row 1.

**ROW 21 (RS)** Ch 1, sc in first 12 sts, hdc in next 12 sts, dc in next 12 sts, tr in next 12 sts, turn.

**ROW 22** Ch 4 (counts as 1 tr), skip first st, tr in next 11 sts, dc in next 12 sts, hdc in next 12 sts, sc in last 12 sts. Break B and join D.

**ROWS 23 AND 24** With D, work rows 21 and 22. Break D and join E.

**ROWS 25 AND 26** With E, work rows 21 and 22. Break E and join F.

**ROWS 27 AND 28** With F, work rows 21 and 22. Break F and join C.

**ROWS 29 AND 30** With C, work rows 21 and 22. Break C and join A.

**ROW 31** With A, work row 21.

## LEFT ARMHOLE OPENING/LEFT BACK

**ROW 32** Ch 4 (counts as 1 tr), skip first st, tr in next 11 sts, dc in next 12 sts, hdc in next 12 sts, turn, leaving rem sts unworked. Break A and join B.

**ROW 33** With B, ch 1, hdc in next 12 sts, dc in next 12 sts, tr in next 12 sts, turn.

**ROW 34** Ch 4 (counts as 1 tr), skip first st, tr in next 11 sts, dc in next 12 sts, hdc in next 12 sts. Break B and join D.

**ROWS 35 AND 36** With D, work rows 33 and 34. Break D and join E.

**ROWS 37 AND 38** With E, work rows 33 and 34. Break E and join A.

**ROWS 39 AND 40** With A, work rows 33 and 34. Fasten off.

## FINISHING

Sew center back seam, leaving last 12 sts at top back open.

## LEFT BACK PLACKET EDGING

With RS facing, attach F with a sl st to first st of left back. Ch 2, dc in first 12 sts of left back. Fasten off.

## RIGHT BACK PLACKET EDGING

With RS facing, attach F with a sl st to top of back seam. Ch 2, dc in last 12 sts of right back. Fasten off.

Sew snaps to placket, positioning left back placket over right back placket. Sew 3 miniature doll buttons to RS of left back placket.

## COLLAR

With E, ch 58.

**ROW 1** Sc in 2nd ch from hook, sc in next ch, *ch 1, skip next ch, sc in next 3 ch; rep from * to last 3 ch, skip next ch, sc in last 2 ch, turn.

**ROW 2** Ch 3 (counts as 1 dc), skip first st, dc next st, *ch 1, dc in next 3 sts; rep from * to last 2 sts, dc in last 2 sts to end, turn. Break E and join F.

**ROW 3** With F, ch 1, sc in first 2 sts, *ch 1, sc in next 3 sts; rep from * to last 2 sts, sc in last 2 sts, turn.

**ROW 4** With F, work row 2. Break F and join C.

**ROW 5** With C, ch 1, sc in first 2 sts, tr into ch-1 sp of row 2, *sc in next st, ch 1, skip next st, sc in next st, tr into next ch-1 sp of row 2; rep from * to last 2 sts, sc in last 2 sts, turn.

**ROW 6** Ch 3 (counts as 1 dc), skip first st, dc in next 3 sts, *ch 1, dc in next 3 sts; rep from * to last st, dc in last st. Break C and join B.

**ROW 7** With B, ch 1, sc in next 2 sts, *ch 1, sc in next st, tr into ch-1 sp of row 5, sc in next st; rep from * to last 3 sts, ch 1, skip next st, sc in last 2 sts, turn.

**ROW 8** Ch 3 (counts as 1 dc), skip first st, dc in next sc, *ch 1, dc in next 3 sts; rep from * to last 2 sts, ch 1, dc in last 2 sts. Fasten off.

With RS facing, attach B with a slip st to last st of row 1.

**ROW 9** With B, ch 3 (counts as 1 dc), skip first st, dc in next st, *ch 1, dc in next 3 sts; rep from * to last 2 sts, dc in last 2 sts, turn.

**ROW 10** Ch 1, sl st in first 2 sts, tr into ch-1 sp of row 1, *sc in next st, ch 1, skip next st, sc in next st, tr into next ch-1 sp of row 1; rep from * to last 2 sts, sl st in next st. Fasten off.

## FINISHING

Lay dress flat with back facing. With RS facing, place side edges of collar to back neck edges and sew in position. Fold collar in half, matching center of collar with center front. Sew collar to front neck along center line of collar. Sew rem 9 buttons down center front, using photo as a guide.

## HANDBAG

With B, ch 16.

**ROW 1** Dc in 2nd ch from hook and each in ch across, turn—15 sts.

**ROWS 2–5** Ch 2, dc in each dc across, turn. Break B and join C.

**ROWS 6–9** With C, ch 2, dc in each dc across, turn. Break C and join A.

**ROWS 10–18** With A, ch 2, dc in each dc across, turn. Fasten off.

### FINISHING

HANDLES

With RS facing, attach B with a slip st to 5th st along first row of handbag, ch 10, skip next 5 sts, sl st into next st along first row of handbag. Rep for last row of handbag—2 handles.

Fold WS tog where A and C meet. With back of handbag facing, attach B to lower right corner and work 1 row sc evenly up side edge through both layers to join, turn handbag 90 degrees clockwise and sl st across first 4 sts along top of bag, work 16 sts into ch-10, sl st in last 4 sts along top of bag. Fasten off. With front of handbag facing, attach B to lower right corner and work 1 row sc evenly up side edge through both layers to join, turn handbag 90 degrees clockwise and sl st across first 4 sts along top of bag, work 16 sts into ch-10, sl st in last 4 sts along top of bag. Fasten off.

### EMBROIDERY

With 2 strands of A held together, embroider 5 petals with lazy daisy st on front of handbag. With 2 strands of E held together, make 5 straight sts between the petals and 3 French knots in center of petals. ✿

Every girl needs a bag with flair
to stand out in the crowd!

# Royal Princess

A gown and a crown are all a girl needs to feel like a princess.
Dainty rosebuds dot the skirt and matching purse.

## MATERIALS

- 2 2oz/57g balls (each approx 300yd/274m) of Aunt Lydia's *Bamboo Crochet Thread 10* (bamboo) in #275 coral (A) 🔟
- 1 ball (each approx 100yd/91m) of *Red Heart Fashion Crochet Thread 5* (cotton/metallic) in #410S silver/silver (B) 🔟
- One each sizes B/1 (2.25mm) and D/3 (3.25mm) hook OR SIZE TO OBTAIN GAUGE
- One package Deanna's Vintage Styles beads, or other size 6 beads (approx 1,000)
- One large bead (for crown)
- 3 small snaps

## GAUGE

20 sts and 14 rows = 4"/10cm over FPtr and BPtr using size B/1 (2.25mm) hook.
*Take time to check gauge.*

## STITCH GLOSSARY

**BEG TC (BEG TR CLUSTER)** [Yo twice, insert hook into designated st, yo and draw up a lp, (yo and draw through 2 lps on hook) twice] twice, yo and draw through all 3 lps on hook.
**TC (TR CLUSTER)** [Yo twice, insert hook into designated st, yo and draw up a lp, (yo and draw through 2 lps on hook) twice] 3 times, yo and draw through all 4 lps on hook.

**FPTR (FRONT POST TR)** Yo, insert hook from front to back to front around post of designated st and draw up a lp, [yo and draw through 2 lps] 3 times.
**BPTR (BACK POST TR)** Yo, insert hook from back to front to back around post of designated st and draw up a lp, [yo and draw through 2 lps] 3 times.

## NOTES

**1)** Dress yoke is worked back and forth in rows, from the neckline down, in one piece, leaving side edges open for center back closure.
**2)** Dress top is worked by picking up sts along waist of skirt and is then slip stitched to bottom of yoke, leaving openings for sleeves.
**3)** Skirt is worked back and forth in rows from waist to hem in one piece, leaving side edges open for center back closure and seam.

## DRESS
### YOKE

**NOTE** String 150 beads onto thread A before beginning dress top.
With A, ch 73.

**ROW 1 (RS)** Sc in 2nd ch from hook and each ch across, turn—72 sts.

**ROW 2** Ch 3, Skip first sc, dc in next sc, *slide 1 bead close to hook, ch 2, skip next sc, dc in next sc; rep from * across, turn.

**ROW 3** *Ch 6, skip next ch-2 sp, sc in next dc; rep from * across, turn.

**ROW 4** *Ch 8, sc in next ch-6 sp, ch 1, slide 2 beads, ch 2, sc in next ch-6 sp; rep from * across, turn.

**ROW 5** *Ch 10, sc in next ch-8 sp; rep from * across, turn.

**ROW 6** Ch 3, into each ch-10 sp work [3 sc in sp, (slide one bead, ch 1, sc in sp) 5 times, 2 sc in sp]. Fasten off. Set aside.

## SKIRT

**NOTE** String approx 670 beads onto thread A before beginning skirt.
With A, ch 76.

**ROW 1 (RS)** Dc in 4th ch from hook, *2 dc in next ch, 1 dc in next ch; rep from * to end of ch, turn—109 sts.

**ROW 2** Ch 3 (counts as 1 dc), skip first dc, *work FPtr around next dc, ch 1, skip next dc; rep from * to last 2 sts, work FPtr around next dc, dc into top of beg ch, turn—57 sts.

**ROW 3** Ch 1, sc in first st, *sl 1 bead (ch 2, sc in next ch-1 sp): rep from * to last 2 sts, sc in top of ch-3, turn.

**ROW 4** Ch 3 (counts as 1 dc), BPtr around FPtr, *ch 1, BPtr around next FPtr; rep from * to last st, dc into last sc, turn.

**ROWS 5 AND 7** Ch 1, sc in first st, ch 1, sc in ch-1 sp, *ch 2, sc in ch-1 sp; rep from * to last st, ch 1, sc in last dc.

**ROW 6** Ch 3 (counts as 1 dc), BPtr around next post, *ch 1, BPtr around next post; rep from * to last st, dc into last sc, turn.

**ROW 8** Ch 3 (counts as 1 dc), BPtr around next post, *ch 1, tr in ch-1 sp, ch 1, BPtr around next post; rep from * to last st, dc into last sc, turn.

**ROW 9** Ch 1, sc in first st, ch 1, sc in ch-1 sp, *ch 2, sc in ch-1 sp; rep from * to last st, ch 1, sc in last dc.

**ROW 10** Ch 3 (counts as 1 dc), BPtr around next post, *ch 1, BPtr around next post; rep from * to last st, dc into last sc, turn.

**ROW 11** Rep row 9.
Rep last 2 rows 21 times more, placing beads as given for row 3 on rows 19, 39, 47, 49, 51, and 53. Fasten off.
Sew center back seam of skirt, leaving last 1½"/4cm open for back opening.

## TOP

**NOTE** String approx 40 beads onto thread A before beginning skirt.
With RS of skirt facing, attach yarn with a slip st to first ch of row 1.

**ROW 1 (RS)** Ch 1, work 1 sctbl of each ch to end of row, turn—76 sts.

**ROW 2** Ch 1, work 1 sc first st and in each st across, turn.

**ROW 3** Ch 1, work 1 sc in first st and next 7 sts, *ch 5, skip 4 sts, sc in next st; rep from * to last 8 sts, sc in each st to end, turn.

**ROW 4** Ch 1, sc in first st and next 6 sts, ch 5, *picot [sc, ch 1, slide 1 bead close to hook, ch 2, sc] into 3rd ch of next ch-5 arch, ch 5; rep from * to last 8 sts, skip next 1 st, sc in last 7 sts, turn.

**ROW 5** Ch 1, sc in first st and next 5 sts, ch 5, *skip picot, picot in 3rd ch of next ch-5 arch, ch 5; rep from * to last 7 sts, skip next 1 st, sc in last 6 sts, turn.

**ROW 6** Ch 1, sc in first st and next 4 sts, ch 5, *picot [sc, ch 1, slide 1 bead close to hook, ch 2, sc] into 3rd ch of next ch-5 arch, ch 5; rep from * to last 6 sts, skip next 1 st, sc in last 5 sts, turn.

**ROW 7** Ch 1, sc in first st and next 3 sts, ch 5, *skip picot, picot in 3rd ch of next ch-5 arch, ch 5; rep from * to last 5 sts, skip next 1 st, sc in last 4 sts, turn.

**ROW 8** Ch 2, dc in first st and next 2 sts, ch 5, *picot [sc, ch 1, slide 1 bead close to hook, ch 2, sc] into 3rd ch of next ch-5 arch, ch 5; rep from * to last 4 sts, skip next 1 st, dc in last 3 sts, turn.

## JOIN DRESS TOP AND YOKE

Hold last row of yoke with RS facing.

**ROW 9** Ch 2, dc in first st and next 2 sts, [6 sc in next ch-5 sp, 2 sc in picot ch-3 sp] 3 times (left armhole opening); 3 sc in next ch-5 sp, skip first 6 sc from yoke row 5, sc around next sc of row 5, 3 sc in same ch-5 sp, [3 sc in next ch-5 sp, sc around next sc from yoke row 5, 3 sc in same ch-5 sp] 4 times, [6 sc in next ch-5 sp, 2 sc in picot ch-3 sp] 4 times (right armhole opening), dc in last 3 sts. Fasten off.

Place first inch of beg ch of yoke over dress top, and sew in place. Rep for other end of yoke.

## SLEEVES (MAKE 2)

**NOTE** String approx 80 beads onto thread A before beginning sleeves.

With A, ch 28. Join with a slip st to form a ring.

**RND 1** Ch 2, hdc in first ch and each ch around, join with a slip st to first hdc—28 sts.

**RND 2** Ch 2, dc in first st, *ch 2, slip bead close to hook, ch 1, skip next hdc, 1 dc in next st; rep from * to last st, ch 2, slip bead close to hook, ch 1, join with a slip st in first dc.

**RND 3** Ch 1, sc in first st, ch 5, skip first sp, sc in next sp, *ch 5, skip next sp, sc in next sp; rep from * to last 2 sp's, ch 5, join with a slip st to first sc.

**RND 4** *Ch 3, slip a bead close to hook, ch 3, 1 sc in top of next sp, rep from * around until sleeve measures 2¼"/5.5cm from beg.

## JOIN SLEEVE TO DRESS TOP AND YOKE

**NEXT RND** Hold sleeve in place at armhole, skipping first ch-5 sp of dress top, work ch 3, 1 sc next ch-5 sp of dress top, ch 3, sc in next sp of sleeve, ch 3, 1 sc in 4th ch-10 sp of yoke, [ch 3, sc in next sp of sleeve, ch 3, sc in next ch-10 sp of yoke] twice more, *ch 3, sc in next sp of sleeve, ch 3, sc in next sp of dress top; rep from * around, join with a slip st to beg ch. Fasten off.

Repeat for 2nd sleeve.

## BEADED ROSEBUDS (MAKE 4)

**NOTE** String 10 beads onto thread A for each rose to be made.

With A, ch 9.

**ROW 1** Sc in 2nd ch from hook, 2 sc in each ch across, turn—16 sts.

**ROW 2** Ch 1, 2 sc in each sc across, turn—32 sts.

**ROW 3** Ch 1, 2 sc in each of next 2 sc, *slide 1 bead close to hook, ch 2, skip next sc, 2 sc in next sc; rep from * across. Fasten off.

## NON-BEADED ROSEBUDS (MAKE 8)

With A, ch 9.

**ROW 1** Sc in 2nd ch from hook, 2 sc in each ch across, turn—16 sts.

**ROW 2** Ch 1, 2 sc in each sc across, turn—32 sts.

**ROW 3** Rep row 2. Fasten off.

## FINISHING

### SKIRT SCALLOP

With yarn doubled, bring row 9 of skirt together with row 3 of skirt and tack through both rows, approx 2"/5cm apart. Sew 2 snaps to back opening. Sew 10 of the rosebuds in random pattern to dress, using photo as a guide. Sew remaining 2 rosebuds to dress back over top of snaps.

## CROWN

### SCALLOPS

With size D/3 (3.25mm) hook and B, ch 69.

**ROW 1 (WS)** Beg tr over 5th and 6th ch from hook, *ch 5, 1 dc into last ch of tr just made, 1 tr over next 3 ch, ch 3, 1 tr over next 3 ch; rep from * to last 6 ch, ch 5, 1 dc into last ch of tr just made, 1 tr over next 3 ch, turn.

**ROW 2** Ch 4, tr in next ch-5 sp, [ch 4, tr] twice in same sp, *1 sc in next ch-3 lp, [1 tr, ch 4] twice in next ch-5 sp, 1 tr in same sp; rep from * to end. Fasten off.

## BAND

With RS facing and working along foundation ch, attach yarn to right-hand edge.
**ROW 1** Ch 4, tr in next ch and in each ch to end. Fasten off. Sew snap to side edge of band to close.

## PURSE

With B/1 (2.25mm) hook and A, ch 4. Join with a sl st to form a ring.
**RND 1** Ch 1, 8 sc in ring, join with a sl st to first sc.
**RNDS 2–3** Ch 1, 2 sc in each sc around, join with a sl st to first sc—32 sts.
**RND 4** Ch 2, 1 dctbl in each sc around, join with a sl st to first dc.
**RND 5** Ch 3, 1 tr in each dc around, join with a sl st to first tr.
**RND 6** Ch 3, 1 FPtr in each tr around, join with a sl st to first FPtr.
**RND 7** Ch 3, *skip next FPtr, FPtr around next FPtr, rep from * around, join with a sl st to first FPtr—16 sts.
**RND 8** Ch 1, sc in each st around, join with a sl st to first sc. Fasten off.
Attach 1 non-beaded rosebud to front center of bag, using photo as a guide.

## HANDLE

String 20 beads onto A and sew each end onto top edge on each side of purse opening. ✿

# Dressed Up in Daisies

A cozy turtleneck tunic embroidered with scarlet blossoms is pretty as a picture.

## MATERIALS

- 1 3½oz/100g skein (each approx 437yd/400m) of Cascade Yarns *Heritage Silk Paints* (superwash wool/silk) in #9958 mulberry ⓵
- One each sizes C/2 (2.75mm), D/3 (3.25mm), and F/5 (3.75mm) hooks OR SIZE TO OBTAIN GAUGE
- 1 .18oz/5g skein (each approx 16yd/15m) of *DMC Cotton Perlé 3* (cotton) each in #321 red and #301 black (for embroidery) ⓵
- 5 small black beads
- Stitch markers

## GAUGE

23.5 sts and 28 rows = 4"/10cm over sc using size F/5 (3.75mm) hook.
*Take time to check gauge.*

## FRONT AND BACK (BOTH ALIKE)

With F/5 (3.75mm) hook, ch 51.
**ROW 1** Sc in 2nd ch from hook, sc in each ch to end of ch, ch 1, turn—50 sts.
**ROW 2** Sc in each sc across, ch 1, turn. Rep row 2 until piece measures 6½"/16.5cm from beg. Fasten off.
Place front and back with RS tog. Along one short side, measure 1"/2.5cm from each edge, sew both pieces tog from outer edge to 1"/2.5cm mark for shoulder seams.

## COWL COLLAR

With size C/2 (2.75mm) hook and WS facing, attach yarn to center back and sc 14 sts to right shoulder seam, then sc 20 sts evenly across front, sc 14 sts from left shoulder seam to center back—38 sts. Join rnd with a sl st to first sc, ch 1. Do *not* turn. Work 1 sc in each st for 3 rnds. Change to D/3 (3.25mm) hook and work a further 3 rnds of sc. Change to F/5 (3.75mm) hook and work in rnds of sc until collar measures 4"/10cm. Finish off.

## SLEEVES (MAKE 2)

Place markers 3½"/9cm down from each shoulder on side edge of front and back for armholes. Sew side seams from lower edge to markers. With size F/5 (3.75mm) hook and RS facing, attach yarn with a slip st to side seam. Work 40 sc evenly around armhole opening. Join rnd with a sl st to first sc. Do *not* turn.
**RND 1** Sc2tog, sc in each st to last 2 sts, sc2tog.
Rep rnd 1 until 16 sts rem. Work 5 rnds even. Fasten off.

## FINISHING

Using photo as guide, embroider flowers on front, using straight stitch for black stems and lazy daisy stitch for red petals. Sew bead to each flower center. Gather 1½"/4cm at center front neck and secure. ✿

# Striped Safari

This afghan adorned with leaves and a friendly giraffe is so cute and colorful you'll want to hang it on your wall.

**FINISHED MEASUREMENTS**
Approx 13½"/34.5cm x 16 ½"/42cm

**MATERIALS**
- 1 1¾oz/50g skein (each approx 273yd/250m) of Cascade Yarns *220 Fingering* (wool) each in #7824 burnt orange (A), #7827 goldenrod (B), #8910 citron (C), and #8908 anis (D) ⬤
- Small amount of black embroidery floss
- Size E/4 (3.5mm) crochet st afghan hook OR SIZE TO OBTAIN GAUGE
- Size E/4 (3.5mm) hook
- Tapestry needle

**GAUGE**
24 sts and 24 rows = 4"/10 cm over afghan st using size E/4 (3.5mm) crochet afghan st hook.
*Take time to check gauge.*

**STITCH GLOSSARY**
**AFGHAN ST** Ch number of sts in pat.
**ROW 1** Insert hook in 2nd ch from hook/st, yo, draw lp through and leave on hook. *Insert hook into next ch/st, yo, draw lp through and leave on hook; rep from * to end. Do not turn.
**ROW 2** Reverse: yo, draw through 1 lp, *yo, draw through 2 lps; rep from * until only 1 lp rem on hook. do not turn.

**CROSS ST OVER AFGHAN ST**
To cross st, thread a length of yarn onto a tapestry needle. Insert the needle from back to front at the bottom-left corner of st and draw the needle up. Insert the needle at the top-right corner of the same stitch, angled vertically down. Bring the needle out at the bottom-right corner of the same st and draw the yarn through. Rep the two preceding steps across the row in the sts where the chart calls for cross-stitching. Insert your needle at the top-left corner of the same st you ended the first half with, angled vertically down. Bring the needle out at the bottom-left corner of the same st and draw the yarn through. Rep the two preceding steps across the row, completing each cross-st.

**AFGHAN**
With C, ch 80 sts and work afghan st for 6 rows, switch to D and work afghan st for 6 rows. Cont in this stripe pat, alternating C and D, until there are 9 C stripes and 8 D stripes completed. Fasten off.

**FINISHING**
UPPER/LOWER EDGING
With crochet hook, RS facing and C, work 1 row sc evenly along top edge of afghan. Fasten off. Rep for lower edge.

EMBROIDERY
Working cross st over afghan st, embroider giraffe, following chart. (Farthest right cross stitch— the giraffe tail—should be 5 sts from right edge of afghan. See chart for vertical placement in relation to stripes.)
With A, cut 44 4"/10cm lengths. With crochet hook and 3 strands held tog, hook 13 fringes to neck of giraffe, using photo as a guide for placement. Using 5 strands held tog, hook to end of embroidered tail.

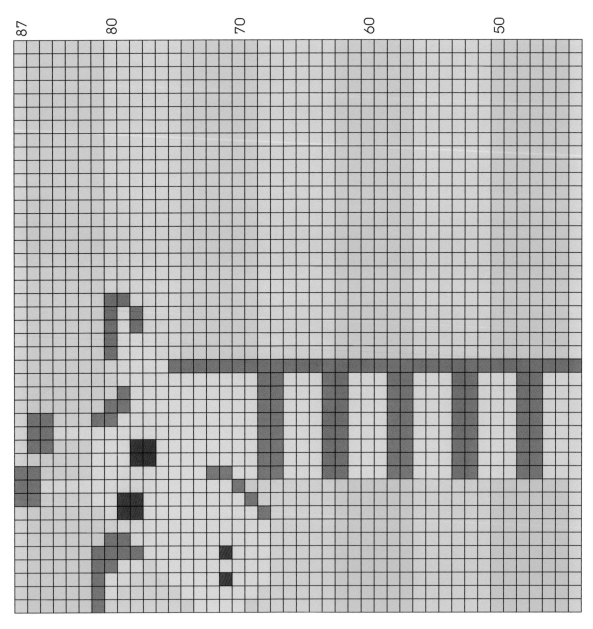

## Color Key
- 🟧 Burnt orange (A)
- ⬜ Goldenrod (B)
- ⬜ Citron (C)
- ⬜ Anise (D)
- ⬛ Black

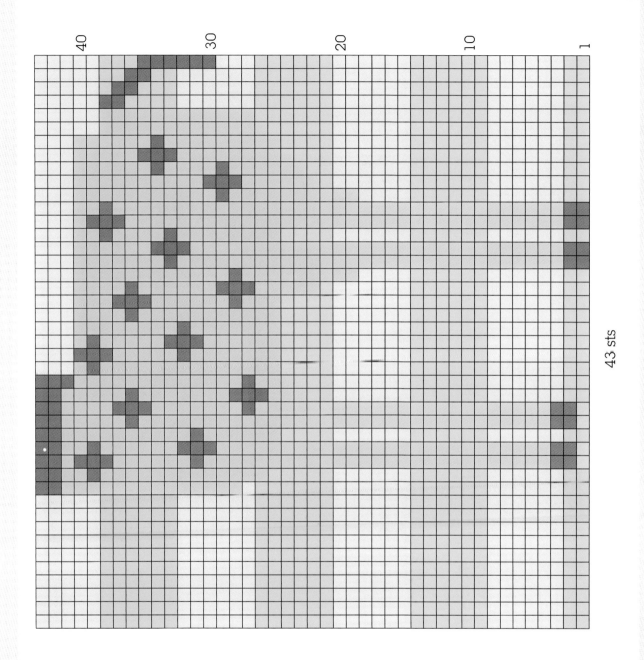

43 sts

## LEAVES

**NOTE** Make 5 large C with stems, 6 large C without stems, 2 large B with stems, 3 large B without stems, 1 large A with stem, 8 small A without stems, 8 small C with stems, 2 small C without stems, 5 small B without stems.

### LARGE LEAF
Ch 14.

**RND 1** Sl st in 2nd ch from hook, sc in next 3 ch, hdc in next 2 ch, dc in next 3 ch, 2 hdc in next 2 ch, sc in next ch, 3 sc in last ch (working around to other side of foundation ch), sc in next ch, hdc in next 2 ch, dc in next 3 ch, hdc in next 2 ch, sc in next 3 ch, sl st in last ch. Fasten off.

### CENTER RIB AND STEM
Working along foundation ch on RS of leaf, sl st in each ch to end, ch 6 for stem. Fasten off.

### SMALL LEAF
Ch 8.

**RND 1** Sl st in 2nd ch from hook, sc in next ch, hdc in next ch, dc in next ch, hdc in next ch, sc in next ch, 3 sc in last ch (working around to other side of foundation ch), sc in next ch, hdc in next ch, dc in next ch, hdc in next ch, sc in next ch, sl st in last 2 ch. Fasten off.

### CENTER RIB AND STEM
Working along foundation ch on RS of leaf, sl st in each ch to end. Ch 6 for stem. Fasten off. Sew leaves to afghan, using photo as a guide for edging and appliqué placement. ✿

# Irish Eyes

Travel in style to the Emerald Isle—or anywhere else—
in a double-breasted coat and jaunty cap.

## MATERIALS

- 2 1¾oz/50g balls (each approx 180yd/165m) of Grignasco *Champagne* (merino/silk) in #1110 green ②
- Size D/3 (3.25mm) hook OR SIZE TO OBTAIN GAUGE
- Stitch markers
- 8 ⅜"/1cm buttons (JBH #92918 Kerry gunmetal used in sample)
- Purchased pin (optional—for hat)

## GAUGE

20 sts and 16 rows = 4"/10cm over hdc using size D/3 (3.25mm) hook. *Take time to check gauge.*

## STITCH GLOSSARY

**DC2TOG** [Yo, insert hook and draw up a lp, yo and draw through 2 lps on hook] twice, yo and draw through all 3 lps on hook.

**FPDC (FRONT POST DC)** Yo, insert hook from front to back to front around post of designated st and draw up a lp, [yo and draw through 2 lps] twice.

## NOTE

Left front/back and right front/back of coat are worked horizontally as panels to underarm side edge, leaving opening for armholes. Sts are then worked toward center back/front, and then left and right pieces are seamed at center back to join.

## COAT

### RIGHT FRONT AND BACK SIDE PANEL

Ch 91.
**ROW 1** Sc in 2nd ch from hook and in each ch to end—90 sts. Do not turn.
**ROW 2** Ch 1, work in rev sc tfl in each sc across. Do not turn.
**ROWS 3 AND 4** Ch 1, hdc tbl in each st across, turn.
**ROW 5** Ch 1, hdc in each hdc across. Do not turn.
**ROW 6** Ch 1, work in rev sc in both lps of hdc across. Do *not* turn.
**ROW 7** Ch 1, hdc around post in row 6 to last 18 sts, turn, leaving rem 18 sts unworked for right side vent.
**ROW 8** Ch 1, hdc between each st across, turn.

### DIVIDE FOR RIGHT ARMHOLE

**ROWS 9, 11, AND 13** Ch 1, hdc between each of next 32 hdc, turn, leaving rem sts unworked for right armhole and front.
**ROWS 10 AND 12** Ch 1, hdc between each st to armhole, turn.
**ROW 13** Ch 1, hdc between next 18 sts, ch 1, do not turn, rev sc in last 18 sts worked. Fold piece in half with RS together, and sl st next 14 sts together with matching 14 sts from last row worked for front, leaving rem sts open for armhole. Fasten off.

### CENTER RIGHT BACK

**ROW 1** With RS facing, attach yarn with a slip st to first sc at lower front edge, ch 1, 1 hdc tbl in same st as sl st and each st to end of row, turn.

**ROW 2** Ch 1, hdc between next 40 sts, turn, leaving rem sts for neck and front unworked.
**ROW 3** Ch 1, hdc between each st to end of row, do not turn, rev sc tfl in last 18 sts worked. Fasten off.

## CENTER RIGHT FRONT

**ROW 1** With RS facing, attach yarn with a slip st to first hdc at lower front edge, ch 1, hdc between next 40 sts, turn.
**ROWS 2–5** Ch 1, hdc between each st across, turn. Fasten off.

## LEFT FRONT AND BACK
Ch 91.

**ROW 1** Sc in 2nd ch from hook and in each ch to end—90 sts. Do not turn.
**ROW 2** Ch 1, work in rev sc tfl in each sc across. Do not turn.
**ROWS 3 AND 4** Ch 1, hdc tbl in each st across, turn.
**ROW 5** Ch 1, hdc in each hdc across. Do not turn.
**ROW 6** Ch 1, work in rev sc in both lps of hdc across. Fasten off.
**ROW 7** With RS facing, skip first 18 sts, attach yarn with a sl st to next st, ch 1, hdc around post in row 6 of same st as sl st and each st across, turn.
**ROW 8** Ch 1, hdc between each st across. Fasten off.

## DIVIDE FOR LEFT ARMHOLE

**ROW 9** With RS facing, skip first 58 sts (14 sts side seam, 26 sts left armhole), attach yarn with a sl st to next st, ch 1, hdc between next hdc and between each st across, turn—32 hdc.
**ROWS 10 AND 12** Ch 1, hdc between each st across, turn.
**ROW 11** Ch 1, hdc between each st across, turn.
Row 13 Ch 1, hdc between each st across, do not turn, rev sc in last 18 sts worked.
Fold piece in half with RS together, and sl st next 14 sts together with matching 14 sts from last row worked for front, leaving rem sts open for armhole. Fasten off.

## CENTER LEFT FRONT

**ROW 1** With RS facing, attach yarn with a slip st to first sc at lower back edge, ch 1, 1 hdc tbl in same st as sl st and each st to end of row, turn.
**ROW 2** Ch 1, hdc between next 40 sts, turn, leaving rem sts for neck and back unworked.
**ROWS 3–5** Ch 1, hdc between each st across, turn. Fasten off.

## CENTER RIGHT BACK

**ROW 1** With RS facing, attach yarn with a slip st to first hdc at lower back edge, ch 1, hdc between next 40 sts, turn.
**ROW 2** Ch 1, hdc between each st across, do not turn, rev sc tfl across. Fasten off.

## SLEEVES

With RS facing, attach yarn with a sl st to center st of underarm.
**RND 1** Ch 1, work 33 sc evenly around armhole opening, join with a sl st to first sc—33 sts.
**RNDS 2 AND 3** Ch 2, hdc in each st around, join with a sl st to first st.
**RNDS 4–11** Ch 2, hdc2tog, hdc in each st around to last 2 sts, hdc2tog, join with a sl st to first st—17 sts.
**RNDS 12–17** Ch 2, hdc in each st around, join with a sl st to first st.
**ROW 18** Ch 1, work rev sc in each st around, join with a sl st to first st. Fasten off.

## FINISHING

Sew center back seam, leaving last 18 sts open for center back vent.

## COLLAR

With WS facing, attach yarn with a slip st to center front edge at neck.
**ROW 1 (WS)** Ch 1, work 35 sc evenly around neck opening, turn.
**ROW 2** Ch 1, hdc in each sc, turn.
**ROW 3** Ch 1, hdc tfl in each st across, do not turn.
**ROW 4** Ch 1, work in rev sc in both lps of hdc across. Do not turn.
**ROW 5** Ch 1, hdc around post in row 4 across, turn.
**ROW 6** Ch 1, hdc tfl in each st across, do not turn.
**ROW 7** Ch 1, work in rev sc in both lps of hdc across. Fasten off.

## PLACKET
Ch 9.

**ROW 1** Hdc in 2nd ch from hook and each ch to end, turn.

**ROW 2** Ch 2, hdc in each st across. Do not turn. Work 1 row rev sc around, join with a sl st to first st. Fasten off.

Attach placket to center back of coat by sewing on 2 buttons through both layers to secure. Using photo as a guide, sew buttons to front of coat.

## HAT
Ch 4. Join with sl st to form a ring.

**RND 1** Ch 3 (counts as 1 dc), 1 dc into ring, [ch 2, 2 dc in ring] 5 times, ch 2, join with a sl st to top of beg ch-3.

**RND 2** Ch 3 (counts as 1 dc), 2 dc in same st as sl st, 1 dc in next dc, *ch 3, skip next ch-2 sp, 3 dc into next dc, 1 dc in next dc; rep from * 4 more times, ch 3, skip next ch-2 sp, join with a sl st to top of beg ch-3.

**RND 3** Ch 3 (counts as 1 dc), 2 dc into same st as sl st, 1 dc in next dc, dc2tog over next 2 dc, *ch 4, skip next ch-3 sp, 3 dc into next dc, 1 dc into next dc, dc2tog over next 2 dc, rep from * 4 more times, ch 4, skip next ch-3 sp, join with a sl st to top of beg ch-3.

**RND 4** Ch 3 (counts as 1 dc), 2 dc in same st as sl st, [1 dc into next dc] twice, dc2tog over next 2 dc, *ch 5, skip next ch-4 sp, 3 dc in next dc, [1 dc into next dc] twice, dc2tog over next 2 dc; rep from * 4 more times, ch 5, skip next ch-4 sp, join with a sl st to top of beg ch-3.

**RND 5** Ch 3 (counts as 1 dc), 2 dc in same st as sl st, [1 dc in next dc] 3 times, dc2tog over next 2 dc, *ch 6, skip next ch-5 sp, 3 dc in next dc, [1 dc in next dc] 3 times, dc2tog over next 2 dc; rep from * 4 more times, ch 6, skip next ch-5 sp, join with a sl st to top of beg ch-3.

**RND 6** Ch 3 (counts as 1 dc), 2 dc in same st as sl st, [1 dc in next dc] 4 times, dc2tog over next 2 dc, *ch 7, skip next ch-6 sp, 3 dc in next dc, [1 dc in next dc] 4 times, dc2tog over next 2 dc; rep from * 4 more times, ch 7, skip next ch-6 sp, join with a sl st to top of beg ch-3.

**RND 7** Ch 3 (counts as 1 dc), 2 dc in same st as sl st, [1 dc in next dc] 5 times, dc2tog over next 2 dc, *ch 8, skip next ch-7 sp, 3 dc in next dc, [1 dc in next dc] 5 times, dc2tog over next 2 dc; rep from * 4 more times, ch 8, skip next ch-7 sp, join with a sl st to top of beg ch-3.

**RND 8** Ch 3 (counts as 1 dc), *skip first dc, 1 dc in next dc, [dc2tog over next 2 dc] 4 times, 4 dc into ch-8 sp; rep from * 4 times more, join with a sl st to top of beg ch-3.

**RND 9** Ch 3 (counts as 1 dc), skip first dc, 1 dc in next dc, *dc2tog over next 2 dc; rep from * around, join with a sl st to top of beg ch-3.

**RND 10** Ch 3 (counts as 1 dc), skip first dc, 1 dc in each dc around, join with a sl st to top of beg ch-3.

**RND 11** Ch 3, 1 dc in same st as sl st, 1 dc in next dc, *2 dc in next dc, 1 dc in next dc; rep from * around, join with a sl st to top of beg ch-3.

**RND 12** Ch 3 (counts as 1 dc), *1 fpdc around next dc, 1 dc in next dc; rep from * around. Fasten off. ✿

# Pretty as a Picture

A loop-stitch skirt, a top with dainty buttons and ruffles, and a matching circle purse are a true work of art.

## MATERIALS

- 2 2.8oz/80g packages of 8 skeins (each 28yd/26m) of Lion Brand Yarn *Bonbons* (cotton) in #601-640 nature
- One each sizes C/2 (2.75mm) and F/5 (3.75mm) hooks OR SIZE TO OBTAIN GAUGE
- 5 small corresponding buttons
- 4 snap fasteners

## GAUGE

24 sts and 12 rows = 4"/10cm over dc using size F/5 (3.75mm) hook. *Take time to check gauge.*

## STITCH GLOSSARY

**FPDC (FRONT POST DC)** Yo, insert hook from front to back to front around post of designated st and draw up a lp, [yo and draw through 2 lps] twice.

**BPDC (BACK POST DC)** Yo, insert hook from back to front to back around post of designated st and draw up a lp, [yo and draw through 2 lps] twice.

**LOOP (FUR) STITCH**
Worked on WS rows, using left-hand finger to control size of loop, insert hook into stitch, wrap yarn around left-hand finger, pick up both yarns of the loop and draw through the stitch, wrap working yarn over hook and draw through all loops on hook.

## SKIRT STRIPE PATTERN

Work 2 rows F, 2 rows B, 2 rows F, 2 rows H, 2 rows F, cont with B.

## NOTES

**1)** Colors used are green (A), pink (B), lavender (C), purple (D), yellow (E), dark brown (F), cream (G), and tan (H).
**2)** Vest is worked sideways in one piece, starting at left front and ending at right front.

## SKIRT

With size F/5 (3.75mm) hook and H, ch 58.
**ROW 1 (RS)** Dc in 4th ch from hook and in each ch across, turn—56 dc.
**ROW 2** Ch 1, sc in next 2 dc, *work loop st over next 4 dc**, sc in next 4 dc; rep from * ending last rep at **, sc in last 2 dc, turn.

**ROW 3** Ch 3 (counts as 1 dc), sk first st, dc in each st to end of row, turn.

Working in skirt stripe pat, rep last 2 rows 6 times more.

**ROW 16** Ch 2, dc in each st to end of row, turn.

**ROW 17** Ch 2, hdc in each st to end of row. Fasten off.

### FINISHING

Sew center back seam, leaving first ¾"/2cm open at hem and last 1½"/4cm open at waist. With 2 strands of B held together, weave strands through last row worked at top of skirt waist and again through last dc row worked. Gather slightly to fit around doll's waist and tie strands into a knot. Sew 1 snap fastener to back waist opening for skirt closure. Cut loops evenly to resemble "fur."

### VEST

#### LEFT FRONT

With F/5 (3.75mm) hook and G, ch 10.

**ROW 1 (RS)** Dc in 2nd ch from hook and each ch across, turn—9 sts.

**ROWS 2–6** Ch 2, dctbl in each dc to end of row, turn.

#### LEFT STRAP

**ROW 7** Ch 2, dctbl in each dc to end of row, ch 14 for left strap, sl st to top of last st of row 1, ch 3, sl st to last ch of beg ch, turn.

**ROW 8** Dc in each of 14 ch for left strap, dctbl of last 9 sts, turn.

#### BACK

**ROW 9** Ch 2, dctbl in first 12 dc, turn, leaving rem sts unworked—12 sts.

**ROWS 10–12** Ch 2, dctbl in next 12 dc, turn.

#### RIGHT STRAP

**ROW 13** Ch 2, dctbl in next 12 dc, ch 17, turn.

**ROW 14** Dc in 4th ch from hook and next 13 sc, dctbl in last 12 dc, turn.

#### RIGHT FRONT

**ROW 15** Ch 2, dctbl in next 9 sts, turn, leaving rem sts unworked—9 sts.

**ROWS 16–19** Ch 2, dctbl in next 9 sts, turn.

**ROW 20** Ch 2, being careful not to twist sts, sl st into top of last dc of right strap, dctbl in 9 right front sts, turn.

**ROW 2** Ch 2, dctbl in next 9 sts, sl st into last ch of right strap. Fasten off.

With RS facing, join G with a sl st to left front bottom corner. Work 1 row sc evenly along bottom of piece to right front bottom corner. Fasten off.

#### RIGHT FRONT RUFFLES

With C/2 (2.75mm) hook and WS facing, attach color F to front loop of 11th st/ch from bottom of right center front (2nd ch of right strap).

**ROW 1** Ch 1, sc in same st, *4 dc in next front loop of st/ch, sc in front loop of next st/ch; rep from * to end, turn—5 scallops per ruffle.

**ROW 2** Ch 2, dctbl of same 11 st/ch. Fasten off.

**ROWS 3 AND 4** With WS facing, attach H to front loop of first st of row 2. Rep rows 1 and 2. Fasten off. With RS facing, join B with a sl st to last sc of row 3. Sl st in first sc, *sl st in next 4 dc, sl st in next sc; rep from * to end of ruffle. Fasten off.

**ROWS 5 AND 6** With WS facing, attach F to front loop of first st of row 4. Rep rows 1 and 2. Fasten off.

#### LEFT FRONT RUFFLES

With C/2 (2.75mm) hook and WS facing, attach color F to front loop of first dc at bottom of left center front.

**ROW 1** Ch 1, sc in same st, *4 dc in next front loop of st/ch, sc in front loop of next st/ch; rep from * to end, turn—5 scallops per ruffle.

**ROW 2** Ch 2, dctbl of same 11 st/ch. Fasten off.

**ROWS 3 AND 4** With WS facing, attach H to front loop of first st of row 2. Rep rows 1 and 2. Fasten off. With RS facing, join B with a sl st to last sc of row 3. Sl st in first sc, *sl st in next 4 dc, sl st in next sc; rep from * to end of ruffle. Fasten off.

**ROWS 5 AND 6** With WS facing, attach F to front loop of first st of row 4. Rep rows 1 and 2. Fasten off.

Sew 5 small buttons to right front, using photo as a guide. Sew 3 snaps to fronts, placing right front over left front.

## PURSE

### FRONT MEDALLION

With F/5 (3.75mm) hook and C, ch 8. Join with a slip st to form a ring.

**RND 1** Ch 4 (counts as 1 dc, ch 1), [2 dc into ring, ch 1] 4 times, 1 dc into ring, join with a slip st to 3rd ch of beg ch-4. Fasten off.

**RND 2** Join B into any ch-1 sp, ch 3 (counts as 1 dc), *fpdc around each of next 2 sts, [dc, ch 1, dc] into next ch-1 sp; rep from * 4 times more, fpdc around each of next 2 sts, dc in first ch-1 sp, ch 1, join with a slip st to top of beg ch-3. Fasten off.

**RND 3** Join D and rep rnd 2. Fasten off.

**RND 4** Join F into any ch-1 sp, ch 3 (counts as 1 dc), *fpdc around each of next 2 sts, [dc, ch 2, dc] into next ch-1 sp; rep from * 4 times more, fpdc around each of next 2 sts, dc in first ch-1 sp, ch 2, join with a slip st to top of beg ch-3. Fasten off.

**RND 5** Join H into any ch-2 sp, ch 4 (counts as 1 dc, ch 1), *fpdc around each of next 2 sts, ch 1, [dc, ch 2, dc] into next ch-2 sp, ch 1; rep from * 4 times more, fpdc around each of next 2 sts, ch 1, dc in first ch-2 sp, ch 2, join with a slip st to 3rd ch of beg ch-3. Fasten off.

**RND 6** Join G into any ch-2 sp, ch 4 (counts as 1 dc, ch 1), dc in next ch-1 sp, ch 1, *fpdc around each of next 2 sts, ch 1, dc in next ch-1 sp, ch 1, [dc, ch 2, dc] into next ch-2 sp, ch 1, dc in next ch-1 sp, ch 1; rep from * 4 times more, fpdc around each of next 2

sts, ch 1, dc in next ch-1 sp, dc in first ch-2 sp, ch 2, join with a slip st to 3rd ch of beg ch-3. Fasten off.

**RND 7** Join F into any ch-2 sp, ch 3 (counts as 1 dc), *dc in next ch-1 sp, ch 1, dc in next ch-1 sp, fpdc around each of next 2 sts, dc in next ch-1 sp, ch 1, dc in next ch-1 sp, [dc, ch 2, dc] in next ch-2 sp; rep from * 4 times, dc in next ch-1 sp, ch 1, dc in next ch-1 sp, fpdc around each of next 2 sts, dc in next ch-1 sp, ch 1, dc in next ch-1 sp, dc in first ch-2 sp, ch 2, join with a slip st to top of beg ch-3. Fasten off.

### BACK MEDALLION

With H only, work rnds 1–6 as given for front medallion. Fasten off.

**RND 7** Join F into any corner ch-2 sp and work rnd 7 as given for front medallion. Fasten off.

### FINISHING

Place wrong sides of medallions together. Attach F with a slip st to any st. Leaving a 2"/5cm opening, sl st medallions together. Do not cut yarn. Ch 20 (for handle), sl st to opposite side of medallion over 2"/5cm opening to secure, work 1 dc in each ch across to opposite side of opening and sl st to beg st. Fasten off. ✿

# Wrapped in Ruffles

A pretty party dress with a delicate rose and sparkly sequins makes any occasion more festive.

## MATERIALS

- 1 .88oz/25g ball (each approx 137yd/125m) of Schulana Kid-Paillettes (mohair/polyester/silk) each in #320 silver sequins (A) and #310 white sequins (B) ⓪
- Size D/3 (3.25mm) hook OR SIZE TO OBTAIN GAUGE
- 3 snaps
- 24"/61cm ribbon, ¼"/64mm wide
- One purchased rose
- Small amount elastic thread

## GAUGE

24 sts and 16 rows = 4"/10cm over dc using size D/3 (3.25mm) hook. *Take time to check gauge.*

## NOTE

Dress top is worked from the top down.

## STITCH GLOSSARY

**BEG TC (BEG TR CLUSTER)** [Yo twice, insert hook into designated st, yo and draw up a lp (yo and draw through 2 lps on hook) twice], yo and draw through all 3 lps on hook.

**TC (TR CLUSTER)** [Yo twice, insert hook into designated st, yo and draw up a lp, (yo and draw through 2 lps on hook) twice] 3 times, yo and draw through all 4 lps on hook.

## SKIRT

With A, ch 77.

**ROW 1** Dc in 6th ch from hook, *ch 3, sk next 3 ch, dc in next ch; rep from * to end of ch, ch 6, turn—20 dc and 19 sps.

**ROW 2** Dc in next dc, *ch 3, sk ch-3 sp, dc in next dc; rep from * to end of row, ch 3. Do *not* turn.

**ROW 3** Work 5 dc in ch-3 sp of row 1, *ch 1, 6 dc in next ch-3 sp of row 1; rep from * across, end ch 6, turn.

Rep rows 2 and 3 until 10 rows of ruffles are made, end with row 2. Fasten off.

## BODICE

With B, ch 60.

**ROW 1** Dc in 3rd dc from hook, *ch 2, sk next 2 ch, dc in next ch; rep from * to end of ch, ch 4 (counts as ch 2, 1 dc), turn—21 dc and 20 sps.

**ROWS 2 AND 4** Dc in first dc, *ch 2, sk ch-2 sp, dc in next dc; rep from * to end of row, ch 2. Do *not* turn.

**ROWS 3 AND 5** Work 6 dc in 1st ch-2 sp of row 1, *ch 1, 6 dc in next ch-2 sp; rep from * across, ch 2, turn.

**ROW 6** 2 hdc in 1st ch-2 sp, *hdc in next dc, 2 hdc in next ch-2 sp; rep from * to end. Fold in half and mark center. Place markers 9 hdc to right and 9 hdc to left of center.

**ROW 7** Sk all hdc to 1st marker, hdc in st with marker, hdc in each st to 2nd marker, sk all hdc to last hdc, hdc in last st, ch 1, turn—10 sts.

**ROW 8** Hdc in next 10 sts, work 1 hdc in next 4 sts of ruffle, ch 10 for back, ch 1, turn.

**ROW 9** Hdc in each ch of ch-10, work 1 hdc in next 14 sts, work 1 hdc in next 4 sts of ruffle, ch 10, ch 1, turn.

**ROW 10** Hdc in each ch of ch-10, work 1 hdc in each st to end of row, ch 1, turn—38 sts.

**ROW 11** Hdc in each st to end of row, ch 1, turn.
Rep last row for 3¼"/8cm, end with a WS row.

## JOIN BODICE TO SKIRT
Lay right side of top bottom to right side waist of skirt.
**NEXT ROW** With B, work 4 sc in each ch 4 sp of skirt, join with a sl st to first sc. Fasten off.

### FINISHING
Sew skirt center back seam. Sew snaps to back top. Weave ribbon through stitches at waist and tie in bow. Run elastic around top and sleeves, beginning at left back top edge and bottom of first ruffle.
Sew rose to front, using photo as a guide. ✿

A dress that makes her sparkle on her special day—what more could a girl wish for?

# Cowl and Critters

Mix and match these whimsical hats with a color-coordinated cowl to brighten up any ensemble.

## MATERIALS

- 1 2.8oz/80g 8-pack of skeins (each approx 38yd/35m) of Lion Brand Yarn *Bonbons* (acrylic) in #601-620 pastels: light green (A), medium blue (B), sky blue (C), white (D), yellow (E), peach (F), pale pink (G), lavender (H)
- One each sizes D/3 and G/6 (3.25 and 4mm) hooks OR SIZE TO OBTAIN GAUGE
- Small amount of polyester fiberfill
- 2 purchased eyes (optional)

## GAUGE

20 sts and 10 rows = 4"/10cm over dc using size G/6 (4mm) hook. *Take time to check gauge.*

## NOTE

Hats are worked from the top down.

## FROG HAT

With size G/6 (4mm) hook and A, ch 4, join with sl st to 1st ch to form ring.

**RND 1** Ch 3 (counts as 1 dc), 13 sc in ring, join with a sl st to top of beg ch-3—14 dc.

**RND 2** Ch 3 (counts as 1 dc), dc in same dc, 2 dc in each dc across, join with sl st to top of beg ch-28 dc.

**RND 3** Ch 3 (counts as 1 dc), skip first dc, *2 dc in next dc, dc in next dc; rep from * to last dc, 2 dc in last dc, join with a sl st to top of beg ch-3—42 sts.

**RND 4** Ch 3 (counts as 1 dc), skip first dc, dc in next dc, *2 dc in next dc, dc in next 2 dc; rep from * to last dc, 2 dc in last dc, join with a sl st to top of beg ch-3—56 sts.

**RND 5** Ch 3 (counts as 1 dc), skip first dc, dc in each dc around, join with a sl st to top of beg ch-3. Break A and join C.

**RND 6** With C, ch 3 (counts as 1 dc), skip first dc, dc in next 5 dc, *dc2tog, dc in next 6 dc; rep from * to last 2 dc, dc2tog, join with a sl st to top of beg ch-3—49 sts. Break C and join B.

**RND 7** With B, ch 3 (counts as 1 dc), skip first dc, *dc2tog, dc in next 3 dc; rep from * to last 3 dc, dc in last 3 dc, join with a sl st to top of beg ch-3—40 sts. Break B and join A.

**RND 8** With A, ch 1, *sc in next 2 sts, sc2tog; rep from * around, join with a sl st to first sc—30 sts. Fasten off.

## EYES (MAKE 2)

With size G/6 (4mm) hook and B, ch 2.

**RND 1** 6 sc in 2nd ch from hook, join with sl st to first sc. Break B and join D.

**RND 2** With D, work 2 dc in each st around, join with a sl st to first sc—12 sts.

**RNDS 3 AND 4** Sc in each sc around. Stuff with polyester fiberfill.

**RND 5** [Sc2tog] 6 times, join with a sl st to first sc—6 sts.

**RND 6** Sl st in each st around. Fasten off, leaving a sewing tail of 3"/7.5cm.

## EYELIDS (MAKE 2)

With size G/6 (4mm) hook and A, ch 3.

**RND 1** 3 dc in last ch from hook, ch 1, 4 dc in same ch, turn.

**RND 2** Ch 3 (counts as 1 dc), 3 dc in first dc, skip next 3 dc, [3 dc, ch 1, 3 dc] in ch-1 sp, skip next 3 dc, 4 dc in top of beg ch-3. Fasten off, leaving 6"/15cm tail for sewing to top of hat.
Using photo as a guide, sew eyelids to top of hat, centered on each side of beg ring of hat. Place eyes inside lids and sew in place. With D, embroider mouth in stem st.

## COWL

### NET BACKING
With size D/3 (3.25mm) hook and F, ch 78.
**ROW 1** Tr in 6th ch from hook, *ch 3, skip next 3 ch, tr in next ch, rep from * across, turn.
**ROW 2** Ch 6 (counts as 1 tr, ch 3), *skip next ch-3 sp, tr in next tr, ch 3; rep from * to last st, tr in last st. Fasten off.

### FRONT RUFFLES
**ROW 3** With RS facing, attach H to upper right beg corner space of net, ch 3, 2 tr in same sp, *ch 1, 2 tr in next sp, rep from * to last sp, 3 tr in last sp, do not turn, work rev sc into each st and ch-1 sp across, sl st to beg ch-3. Fasten off.
**ROW 4** With RS facing, attach G to same upper right beg corner sp as row 3. Work as given for row 3. Fasten off.

**ROW 5** With RS facing, attach A to next horizontal row of netting and work as given for row 3. Fasten off.
**ROW 6** With RS facing, attach E to same space as A of row 5 and work as given for row 3. Fasten off.
**ROW 7** With RS facing, attach C to last horizontal row of netting and work as given for row 3. Fasten off.
**ROW 8** With RS facing, attach B to same space as C of row 7 and work as given for row 3. Fasten off.

### CORKSCREWS (MAKE 3)
With F, ch 13.
**ROW 1** Work 2 sc in 2nd ch from hook, 2 sc in each ch to end of ch. Fasten off.
Attach corkscrews to center of one side edge of cowl. Gather the other edge and tack under corkscrew edge to make cowl. ✿

## WISE OWL HAT
With size G/6 (4mm) hook and C, foll hat instructions for frog through rnd 8 (working rnds 1–5 and 8 with C and rnds 6–7 with B). Fasten off.

### EYES (MAKE 2)
With size G/6 (4mm) hook and E, ch 3, join with sl st to 1st ch to form ring.
**RND 1** 5 sc in ring, join with a sl st to first sc—5 sts.
**RNDS 2–3** Ch 1, 2 sc in each sc around, join with a sl st to first sc—20 sts. Break E and join B.
**RND 4** With B, 2 sc in each sc around, join with a sl st to first sc—40 sts. Fasten off.

### EARS (MAKE 2)
With size G/6 (4mm) hook, attach C to one side of hat top, work 4 hdc along dc of row 2 of hat.
**ROW 1** Ch 1, skip first hdc, hdc in next 2 hdc, turn—2 sts.
**ROW 2** Ch 1, hdc in first st. Fasten off.
Using photo as a guide, sew eyes to front of hat. Embroider beak using whipstitch, with F. Sew purchased eye centers. ✿

## BUTTERFLY HAT
With size G/6 (4mm) hook and G, foll frog hat instructions through row 8 (working rnds 1–3, 5, and 7 with G and rnds 4, 6, and 8 with H). Fasten off.

## WINGS

Find center of sides by folding hat flat, and mark right and left center. With size G/6 (4mm) hook, work crocodile st along dc already worked on hat as foll:

**1)** With G, work 5 dc down post of row 1 dc before right center mark, ch 1, 5 dc up the post of row 1 dc after right center mark. Fasten off, leaving a tail to tack end down to hat (1 crocodile st made).

**2)** With G, work 1 crocodile st on posts of 2nd and 3rd row 2 dc before right center mark, ch 1, work 1 crocodile st on posts of 2nd and 3rd row 2 dc after right center mark. Fasten off, leaving a tail to tack end down to hat.

**3)** With H, work 1 crocodile st on posts of 5th and 4th row 3 dc before right center mark, ch 1, work 1 crocodile st on posts of first row 3 dc before and after center mark, ch 1, work 1 crocodile st on posts of 4th and 5th row 3 dc after center mark. Fasten off, leaving a tail to tack end down to hat. Tack ends of crocodile sts to hat.

## BODY

With 2 strands of E held together, ch 24.

**ROW 1** 3 sc in 2nd ch from hook, 2 sc in next 19 ch, leave last 4 ch unworked for first antenna, ch 4 for second antenna. Fasten off. Using photo as a guide, with B, embroider 2 French knots for eyes. ✿

## MEOW KITTY HAT

With size G/6 (4mm) hook and D, foll instructions for frog hat through rnd 8, changing to E for rnds 6–8. Fasten off.

### EAR FLAPS AND TIES

Find center of sides by folding hat flat and mark right and left center. With size G/6 (4mm) hook, RS facing and E, count 3 sts each side of right center mark and work 1 dc in these 6 sts, turn—6 sts.
**ROW 2** Hdc2tog, hdc in each of next 2 dc, hdc2tog, turn—4 sts.
**ROW 3** [Hdc2tog] twice, turn—2 sts.
**ROW 4** Hdc2tog, turn.
**ROW 5** Ch 25, turn and sl st in next 25 ch, join with a sl st to last hdc2tog worked. Fasten off. Rep for left center mark.

### EARS

With size G/6 (4mm) hook and D, ch 5.
**ROW 1** Hdc in 2nd ch from hook and each ch to end, turn—4 sts.
**ROW 2** Ch 1, skip first hdc, hdc in next 3 hdc, turn—3 sts.
**ROW 3** Ch 1, skip first hdc, hdc in next 2 hdc, turn—2 sts.
**ROW 4** Ch 1, sc in first 2 sts, work 5 sc evenly along side edge of ear. Fasten off.
Sew ear to center of side, between beg of row 2 and end of row 3. Rep for other ear.
Using C for eyes, B for whiskers, and G for mouth/nose, embroider face, using photo as a guide. ✿

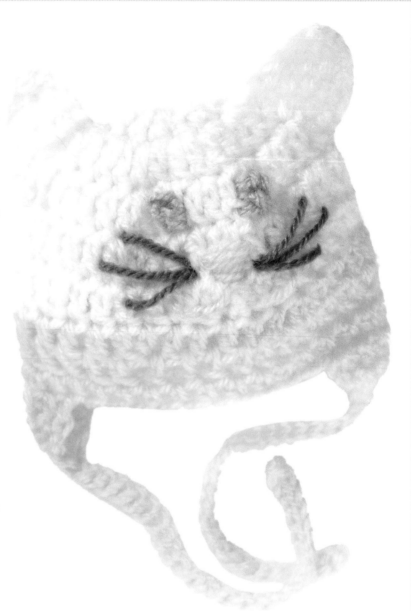

Create your own variations by mixing and matching colors from your yarn pack!

# Chocolate Candy

A coat with scalloped edges, striped bag, and cloche with a flower and a feather are sweet as can be.

## MATERIALS

- 1 1¾oz/50g ball (each approx 208yd/190m) of Knit One Crochet Too *Elfin Tweed* (merino/llama/bamboo/donegal) each in #1837 peach (A), #1261 rose (B), and #1310 taupe (C) (**1**)
- One each sizes C/2 (2.75mm), D/3 (3.25mm), E/4 (3.5mm), and F/5 (3.75mm) hooks OR SIZE TO OBTAIN GAUGE
- ¼"/6mm-wide ribbon in corresponding color, 14"/35.5cm long
- Three ⅝"/15mm buttons (JHB #24496 used in sample)
- 1 bead
- 1 feather (optional)

## GAUGE

20 sts and 20 rows = 4"/10cm over sc using size F/5 (3.75mm) hook. *Take time to check gauge.*

## STITCH GLOSSARY

**FPDC (FRONT POST DC)** Yo, insert hook from front to back to front around post of designated st and draw up a lp, [yo and draw through 2 lps] twice.

**BPDC (BACK POST DC)** Yo, insert hook from back to front to back around post of designated st and draw up a lp, [yo and draw through 2 lps] twice.

**V ST** [Dc, ch 1, dc] in designated st.

## NOTE

Coat is worked in one piece from neck edge down.

## COAT

### BODY

With size C/2 (2.75mm) hook and A, ch 52.

**ROW 1 (RS)** Hdc in 4th ch from hook and each ch across, turn—49 sts. Change to size D/3 (3.25mm) hook.

**ROW 2** Ch 2 (counts as 1 hdc), skip first st, *FPdc around next st, BPdc around next st; rep from * to last 2 sts, FPdc around next st, hdc in last st, turn.

**ROW 3** Ch 2 (counts as 1 hdc), skip first st, *FPdc around next post, BPdc around next post; rep from * to last 2 sts, FPdc around next post, hdc in last st, turn.

**ROW 4** Ch 2 (counts as 1 hdc), skip first st, *FPdc around next post, V st into top of next post; rep from * to last 2 sts, FPdc around next post, hdc in last st, turn.

**ROW 5** Ch 2 (counts as 1 hdc), skip first st, *FPdc around next post, V st in next ch-1 sp; rep from * to last 2 sts, FPdc around next post, hdc in last st, turn. Change to E/4 (3.5mm) hook.

**ROWS 6 AND 7** Ch 2 (counts as 1 hdc), skip first st, *FPdc around next post, [2 dc, ch 1, dc] in next ch-1 sp; rep from * to last 2 sts, FPdc around next post, hdc in last hdc, turn. Change to F/5 (3.75mm) hook.

**ROWS 8 AND 9** Ch 2 (counts as 1 hdc), skip first st, *FPdc around next post, [2 dc, ch 1, 2dc] in next ch-1 sp; rep from * across to last 2 sts, FPdc around next post, hdc in last st, turn.

## ARMHOLE OPENINGS
**ROW 10** Ch 2 (counts as 1 hdc), skip first st, [FPdc around next post, (2 dc, ch 1, 2dc) in next ch-1 sp] 4 times, FPdc around next post, ch 3, skip next 24 sts, FPdc around next post, [(2dc, ch 1, 2 dc) in next ch-1 sp, FPdc around next post] 5 times, ch 3, skip next 24 sts, FPdc around next post, [(2dc, ch 1, 2 dc) in next ch-1 sp, FPdc around next post] 4 times, hdc in last st, turn.

**ROW 11** Ch 2 (counts as 1 hdc), work in established pat across row, working [2 dc, ch 1, 2 dc] into each ch-3 sp for underarm.

**ROW 12** Ch 2 (counts as 1 hdc), skip first st, *FPdc around next post, [2 dc, ch 1, 2dc] in next ch-1 sp; rep from * across to last 2 sts, FPdc around next post, hdc in last st, turn.

**ROW 13** Ch 2 (counts as 1 hdc), skip first st, *FPdc around next post, 6 dc in next ch-1 sp; rep from * to last 2 sts, FPdc around next post, hdc in last st. Fasten off.
With RS facing, join B with a sl st to last st of previous row.

**ROW 14 (RS)** With B, sc in first st, *ch 4, sc in top of FPdc of row 11; rep from * to last st, ch 4, sc in last st, turn.

**ROW 15** Ch 2 (counts as 1 hdc), *[2 dc, ch 1, 2 dc] in next ch-4 sp, FPdc around next sc; rep from * to last ch-4 sp, [2 dc, ch 1, 2 dc]

in last ch-4 sp, hdc in last st, turn.
**ROWS 16 AND 17** Ch 2 (counts as 1 hdc), *[2 dc, ch 1, 2 dc] in next ch-1 sp, FPdc around next post; rep from * to last ch-1 sp, [2 dc, ch 1, 2 dc] in last ch-1 sp, hdc in last st, turn.

**ROW 18** Ch 2 (counts as 1 hdc), skip first st, *6 dc in next ch-1 sp, FPdc around next post; rep from * to last ch-1 sp, 6 dc in last ch-1 sp, hdc in last st. Fasten off.
With RS facing, join C with a sl st to last st of previous row.
**ROWS 19–23** With C, rep rows 14–18. Fasten off.

## SLEEVES
With size F/5 (3.75mm) hook and RS facing, attach A with a sl st into ch-3 sp at left underarm.
**RND 1** *FPdc around next post from row 11, 6 dc in next ch-1 sp; rep from * around sleeve opening, ending last rep working 6 dc into ch-3 sp, join with a sl st to first FPdc. Fasten off.
With RS facing, join B with a sl st to last st of previous row.
**RND 2** With B, sc in first st, *sc in top of FPdc of row 11, ch 4; rep from * around, join with a sl st to first sc.
**RND 3** Ch 2, *FPdc around next sc, [2 dc, ch 1, 2 dc] in next ch-4 sp; rep from * around, join with a sl st to first FPdc.
**RND 4** Ch 2, *FPdc around next post, [2 dc, ch 1, 2 dc] in next ch-1 sp, rep from * around, join with a sl st to first FPdc.
**RND 5** Ch 2, *FPdc around next post, 6 dc in next ch-1 sp; rep

from * around, join with a sl st to first FPdc. Fasten off.
With RS facing, join C with a sl st to last st of previous row.
**RND 6** With C, sc in first st, *sc in top of FPdc of rnd 4, ch 4; rep from * around, join with a sl st to first sc.
**RND 7** Ch 2, *FPdc around next sc, [2 dc, ch 1, 2 dc] in next ch-4 sp; rep from * around, join with a sl st to first FPdc.
**RND 8** Ch 2, *FPdc around next post, 6 dc in next ch-1 sp; rep from * around, join with a sl st to first FPdc. Fasten off.
Rep for right sleeve.

## FINISHING
### CENTER FRONTS/NECK EDGING
With size D/3 (3.25mm) hook and RS facing, attach C with a sl st to bottom corner of right front.
**ROW 1** Work 35 sc evenly up center right front edge, 38 sc along neck opening, and 35 sc evenly down center left front edge. Fasten off.
With size D/3 (3.25mm) hook and RS facing, attach B with a sl st to first sc of edging at bottom corner of right front.
**ROW 2** Ch 1, sctbl in next 15 sc, *ch 6 (button loop), sctbl in next 7 sc, rep from * twice, sctbl in next 8 sc, [4 dctbl in next sc, sctbl in next 2 sc] 12 times, sctbl to end of row. Fasten off.
Sew buttons to left front edging, opposite button loops. Thread ribbon through sts at neck edge and tack ends to WS of coat.

## BAG

With size F/5 (3.75mm) hook and C, ch 4. Join with a sl st in first ch to form a ring.

**RND 1** Ch 1, work 10 sc in ring, join with a sl st to first sc—10 sc.

**RND 2** *Sc in next sc, 2 sc in next sc; rep from * around, join with a sl st to first sc—15 sc.

**RND 3** 2 sc in each sc around, join with a sl st to first sc—30 sc.

**RND 4** 2 sc in first sc, sc in each of next 14 sc, 2 sc in next sc, sc in each of next 14 sc, join with a sl st to first sc—32 sc.

**RND 5** Ch 2, dc in each sc around, join with a sl st to first dc. Break C and join B.

**RND 6** With B, ch 2, dc in each dc around, join with a sl st to first dc.

**RND 7** Ch 2, dc in each dc around, join with a sl st to first dc. Break B and join A.

**RND 8** With A, ch 2, dc in each dc around, join with a sl st to first dc. Break A and join C.

**RNDS 9 AND 10** With C, ch 2, dc in each dc around, join with a sl st to first dc.

**RND 11** *Ch 3, skip 1 st, sc in each of the next 3 dc; rep from * around, join with a sl st to first ch. Break C and join A.

**RND 12** With A, ch 1, *5 dc in ch-3 sp, skip next sc, sc in next sc, skip next sc; rep from * around, join with a sl st to first dc. Fasten off.

### DRAWSTRING

With size F/5 (3.75mm) hook and B, ch 50. Sl st in each ch to end. Fasten off.

Weave drawstring through top of bag and tie knot.

### HAT

With size F/5 (3.75mm) hook and A, ch 6. Join with a sl st to first ch to form a ring.

**RND 1** Ch 1, work 12 sc in ring—12 sc.

**RND 2** Sc tbl in each st around.

**RND 3** 2 sc tbl in each st around—24 sc.

**RND 4** *Sc tbl in each of next 2 sc, 2 sc tbl in next sc; rep from * around—32 sc.

**RND 5** *Sc tbl in each of next 3 sc, 2 sc tbl in next sc; rep from * around—40 sts.

**RND 6** *Sc tbl in each of next 4 sc, 2 sc tbl in next sc—48 sc.

**RNDS 7–12** Sc tbl in each st around. Break A and join C.

**RNDS 13 AND 14** With C, hdc tbl in each st around, join with a sl st to first st. Break C and join A.

**RND 15** Ch 1, *sc in next st, 2 sc in next st; rep from * around, join with a sl st to first sc—72 sts.

**RNDS 16–18** Ch 1, sc in each sc around, join with a sl st to first sc. Fasten off.

### MAIN FLOWER

With size E/4 (3.5mm) hook and B, ch 4. Join with a sl st to first ch to form a ring.

**RND 1** 10 sc in ring, join with a sl st to first sc—10 sc.

**RND 2** *Ch 4, skip next sc, sc in next sc; rep from * around, join with a sl st in 1st ch of beg ch-4.

**RND 3** Ch 1, *[sc, hdc, 2 dc, hdc, sc] in next ch-4 sp; rep from * around, join with a sl st to first sc—6 petals.

**RND 4** *Ch 3, sl st around sc of rnd 2 behind 1st petal made; rep from * around, join with a sl st to first ch.

**RND 5** Ch 1, *[sc, hdc, dc, 2 tr, dc, hdc, sc] in each ch-3 sp; rep from * around, join with sl st to first sc. Fasten off. Leave tail to attach to hat.

### CENTER FLOWER

With size D/3 (3.25mm) hook and C, ch 2.

**RND 1** Work 8 sc in first ch, join with a sl st to first sc.

**RNDS 2–4** Ch 1, sc in each sc around, join with a sl st to first sc.

**RND 5** *Sl st in next sc, skip next sc; rep from * around. Fasten off, leaving sewing tail. Place center flower over center of main flower and sew in position. Sew bead to center flower and sew complete flower to hat, using photo as a guide.

Option: attach purchased feather behind flower. ✿

# Floral Beauty

A casual poncho with a burst of blossoms on the front and a matching cap are just right for spring.

## MATERIALS
- 1.35oz/10g ball (each approx 75yd/69m) of Presencia *Finca Perlé 8* (cotton) each in #113 rose (A), #659 purple (B), #1062 gold (C), and #1734 blue (D)
- Size B/1 (2.25mm) hook OR SIZE TO OBTAIN GAUGE
- 10 corresponding color beads

## GAUGE
28 sts and 16 rows = 4"/10cm over dc using size B/1 (2.25mm) hook. *Take time to check gauge.*

## STITCH GLOSSARY

**DC CLUSTER** Yo, insert hook in st, yo, pull through st, yo, pull through 2 lps on hook, [yo, insert hook in same st, yo, pull through st, yo, pull through 2 lps on hook] 3 times, yo, pull through all 5 lps on hook, ch 1.

**4 DC CLUSTER** [Yo, insert hook in next st, yo, draw yarn through st, yo, draw yarn through 2 lps on hook] 4 times, yo, draw yarn through 5 lps on hook.

**DC2TOG** [Yo, insert hook and draw up a lp, yo and draw through 2 lps on hook] twice, yo and draw through all 3 lps on hook.

## NOTES
1) Poncho is worked in the round from neck down.
2) Hat is worked from brim to crown.

## PONCHO

With D, ch 66. Join with sl st in first ch to form a ring.

**RND 1** Ch 3 (counts as 1 dc), skip first ch, dc in next ch, *ch 1, dc in next 2 ch; rep from * to last ch, skip last ch, ch 1, join with a sl st to top of beg ch-3.

**RND 2** Ch 3 (counts as 1 dc), skip first dc, dc in next st, 2 dc in ch-1 sp, dc in next 2 sts, ch 1, *skip next ch-1 sp, dc in next 2

dc, 2 dc in next ch-1 sp, dc in next 2 dc, ch 1; rep from * to last ch-1 sp, skip last ch-1 sp, join with a sl st to top of beg ch-3.

**RNDS 3–9** Ch 3 (counts as 1 dc), skip first dc, dc in next st, 2 dc in next st, dc in each st to next ch-1 sp, ch 1, skip ch-1 sp, *dc in next 2 sts, 2 dc in next st, dc in each st to next ch-1 sp, ch 1, skip ch-1 sp; rep from * around, join with a sl st to top of beg ch-3. Break D and join C.

**RNDS 10–12** With C, ch 3 (counts as 1 dc), skip first dc, dc in each dc to ch-1 sp, ch 1, skip ch-1 sp, *dc in each st to next ch-1 sp, ch 1, skip ch-1 sp; rep from * around, join with a sl st to top of beg ch-3. Break C and join B.

**RNDS 13–15** With B, rep rnds 10–12. Break B and join A.

**RNDS 16–18** With A, rep rnds 10–12. Fasten off.

## TIE

With D, ch 100. Work 1 sc in 2nd ch from hook and each ch to end of ch. Fasten off.

## FLOWER (MAKE 2 IN B, C, AND D, 3 IN A)

With A, ch 6. Join with sl st to first ch to form a ring.

**RND 1** Ch 5 (counts as 1 dc, ch 2), [dc, ch 2] 7 times into ring, join with a sl st to 3rd ch of beg ch-5.

**RND 2** Ch 3, work dc cluster into next sp, [ch 5, 4 dc cluster in next sp] 7 times, ch 5, sl st to top of beg ch-3. Fasten off.

### FINISHING

Using photo as a guide, attach 9 flowers in a grouping to neck edge of poncho. Sew one bead to each flower center. Weave tie through ch-1 sp's of rnd 1. Attach rem flowers at each end of cord. Sew bead to each flower center.

### HAT

With C, ch 70. Join with sl st in first ch to form a ring.

**RND 1** Ch 3 (counts as 1 dc), skip first ch, dc in next 5 ch, *ch 1, skip next ch, dc in next 6 ch; rep from * to last ch, ch 1, skip last ch, join with a sl st to top of beg ch-3.

**RNDS 2–4** Ch 3 (counts as 1 dc), skip first dc, dc in next 5 sts, *ch 1, skip next ch-1 sp, dc in next 6 sts; rep from * to last ch-1 sp, ch 1, skip last ch-1 sp, join with a sl st to top of beg ch-3. Break C and join B.

**RND 5** With B, work as given for rnd 2.

**RND 6** Ch 3 (counts as 1 dc), skip first dc, dc2tog, dc in next 3 sts, *ch 1, skip next ch-1 sp, dc2tog, dc in next 4 sts; rep from * to last ch-1 sp, ch 1, skip last ch-1 sp, join with a sl st to top of beg ch-3. Break B and join A.

**RND 7** With A, ch 3 (counts as 1 dc), skip first dc, dc in next 4 sts, *ch 1, skip next ch-1 sp, dc in next 5 sts; rep from * to last ch-1 sp, ch 1, skip last ch-1 sp, join with a sl st to top of beg ch-3.

**RND 8** Ch 3 (counts as 1 dc), skip first dc, dc2tog, dc in next 2 sts, *ch 1, skip next ch-1 sp, dc2tog, dc in next 3 sts; rep from * to last ch-1 sp, ch 1, skip last ch-1 sp, join with a sl st to top of beg ch-3. Break A and join C.

**RND 9** With C, ch 3 (counts as 1 dc), skip first dc, dc2tog, dc in next st, *ch 1, skip next ch-1 sp, dc2tog, dc in next 2 sts; rep from * to last ch-1 sp, ch 1, skip last ch-1 sp, join with a sl st to top of beg ch-3.

**RND 10** Ch 3 (counts as 1 dc), skip first dc, dc2tog, *ch 1, skip next ch-1 sp, dc2tog, dc in next st; rep from * to last ch-1 sp, ch 1, skip last ch-1 sp, join with a sl st to top of beg ch-3.

**RND 11** Ch 3 (counts as 1 dc), skip first 2 sts, *ch 1, skip next ch-1 sp, dc2tog; rep from * to last ch-1 sp, ch 1, skip last ch-1 sp, join with a sl st to top of beg ch-3. Break C and join D.

**RND 12** Ch 3 (counts as 1 dc), skip first st, *ch 2, skip next ch-1 sp, dc in next st; rep from * to last ch-1 sp, ch 2, skip last ch-1 sp, join with a sl st to top of beg ch-3.

**RND 13** Ch 3 (counts as 1 dc), *dc in next ch-2 sp; rep from * around; join with a sl st to top of beg ch-3. Fasten off. Sew top of hat closed. ✿

# Let It Snow

Every snowflake is unique, including the one on this pretty pink dress with pearl beads, pockets, and a headband.

## MATERIALS

- 3 balls (each approx 100yd/91m) of Aunt Lydia's *Iced Bamboo 3* (bamboo/metallic) in #3702 pink ice (A) **1**
- 1 .18oz/5g skein (each approx 16yd/15m) of DMC *Coton Perlé 3* (cotton) in #1 blanc (B) **1**
- Size D/3 (3.25mm) hook OR SIZE TO OBTAIN GAUGE
- 2 snap fasteners
- 14 small and 2 medium-size pearl beads

## GAUGE

20 sts and 32 rows = 4"/10cm over sc using size D/3 (3.25mm) hook. *Take time to check gauge.*

## BACK

With A, ch 33.

**ROW 1** Sc in 2nd ch and in each ch across, turn—32 sts.

**ROW 2** Ch 1, sc in each sc across, turn.

Rep row 2 for a total of 36 rows (approx 5"/12.5cm).

### RAGLAN SHAPING

**ROW 37** Sc2tog (dec 1 st), sc in each sc to last 2 sc, sc2tog—30 sts.

Rep last row 9 times more—12 sts.

**ROW 47** Ch 1, sc in next 6 sts, join a 2nd ball of yarn and sc in next 6 sts.

Working both sides at same time, work 5 rows even. Fasten off.

## FRONT

With A, ch 33.

**ROW 1** Sc in 2nd ch and in each ch across, turn—32 sts.

**ROW 2** Ch 1, sc in each sc across, turn.

Rep row 2 for a total of 18 rows.

### BEG CHART

**ROW 19** Ch 1, sc in next 4 sc, work row 1 of chart over next 24 sts, sc in next 4 sc, turn.

Cont as established, working chart to end, then cont with A only, AT THE SAME TIME, shape raglan at each end of chart row 19 and every row to 8 sts. Work even in sc until piece measures same as back. Fasten off.

## SLEEVES (MAKE 2)

With A, ch 23.

**ROW 1** Sc in 2nd ch and each ch across, turn—22 sts.

**ROW 2** Ch 1, sc in each sc across, turn.

Rep last row, inc 1 st each end of next then every 3rd row 4 times more—32 sts. Work even until piece is 4½"/11.5cm from beg.

### RAGLAN SHAPING

**ROW 1** Sl st across next 4 sts, ch 1, sc in same st as last sl st, sc in each sc across to last 3 sts, turn.

**ROW 2** Ch 1, sc2tog, sc in each sc across to last 2 sc, sc2tog, turn.

Rep last row until 16 sts remain. Work even in sc until piece measures 6"/15cm from beg. Fasten off.

## POCKETS (MAKE 2)

With A, ch 13.

**ROW 1** Sc in 2nd ch from hook and in each ch across, turn—12 sts.

**ROW 2** Ch 1, sc in each sc across, turn.

Rep last row 8 times more. Fasten off.

## POCKET EDGING

With RS facing, join B with a sl st to first sc, ch 1, sc in first sc and in next 2 sc, *ch 1, turn, 2 sc in 2nd sc, ch 1, turn, sc in next 3 sc; rep from *, end ch 1, turn, 2 sc in 2nd sc, sl st in last sc.

## FINISHING

Sew raglan sleeve seams. Sew side and sleeve seams, leaving 1"/2.5cm from bottom edge open for side vents. Sew pockets to front, approx 1"/2.5cm from bottom edge, using photo as guide.

## SIDE VENT AND HEM EDGING

With RS facing and A, join with a sl st to right side seam at beg of vent. Work 1 row reverse sc evenly along edges of side vents and hem, join with a sl st to first st. Fasten off.

## NECK EDGING

With RS facing, B, and starting at left back neck edge, work as given for pocket edging to last 4 sts of right back neck edge. Fasten off.

Sew snap fastener to back neck opening, lapping left back over right back. With 8 small beads and 1 medium bead, sew beads to center of snowflake, using photo as a placement guide.

## HEADBAND

With A, ch 70.

**ROW 1** Hdc in 2nd ch from hook and in each ch across, turn— 69 sts.

**ROWS 2 AND 3** Ch 2, hdc in each hdc across, turn.

**ROW 4** Ch 2, hdc in each hdc across, turn work 90 degrees clockwise, work 5 sl sts evenly across side edge, turn work 90 degrees clockwise, *sc in next 3 foundation ch's, ch 1, turn, 2 sc in 2nd sc, turn; rep from * to end of foundation ch, turn work 90 degrees clockwise, work 5 sl sts evenly across side edge, turn work 90 degrees clockwise, *sc in next 3 sc, ch 1, turn, 2 sc in 2nd sc, turn; rep from * to end of row, join with a sl st to first sl st. Fasten off. Sew snap fastener to ends, placing one half on RS of work and one half in corresponding position on WS of work. With 6 small beads and 1 medium bead, sew beads to overlapping end of headband, using photo as a placement guide. ✿

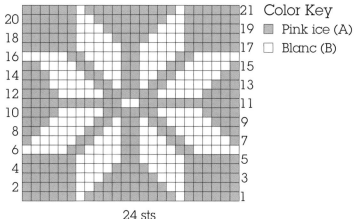

**Color Key**
- ▧ Pink ice (A)
- ☐ Blanc (B)

24 sts

# Walking on Sunshine

Just right for a springtime stroll: a lacy, flowery cardi and capris, with matching clutch, in a mix of neutrals and pastels.

## MATERIALS

- 1 2oz/57g ball (each approx 300yd/274m) of Aunt Lydia's *Bamboo Crochet Thread #10* (viscose from bamboo) each in #0705 pink (A), #0621 key lime (B), #0240 buttercup (C), and #0320 mushroom (D)
- Size B/1 (2.25mm) hook OR SIZE TO OBTAIN GAUGE
- 2 small snaps

## GAUGE

32 sts and 16 rows = 4"/10cm over twin V-stitch using size B/1 (2.25mm) hook. *Take time to check gauge.*

## TWIN V-STITCH

**ROW 1** 2 dc in 5th ch from hook (counts as 1 dc, ch 2), 2 dc in next ch, *skip 2 ch, 2 dc in each of next 2 ch; rep from * to last 2 ch, skip 1 ch, 2 dc in last ch, turn.
**ROW/RND 2** Ch 3 (counts as 1 dc), *skip 2 sts, 2 dc in each of next 2 sts; rep from * to last 2 sts, skip 1 st, dc into 3rd ch of turning ch, turn.
Rep row/rnd 2 for twin V-st.

## NOTES

**1)** Top back is worked from neck/shoulder down.
**2)** Sleeves are picked up and worked down.

## FLOWER MOTIFS (MAKE 4)

With A, ch 6.
**RND 1** [Dc in first ch, ch 2] 3 times, join with a slip st to 4th ch of beg ch-6.
**RND 1** [Sc, hdc, 2 dc, hdc, sc] in 1st ch-2 sp and each ch-2 sp around, join with a slip st to first sc—4 petals.
**RND 2** Working behind petals, *ch 5, skip next 6 sts, sl st in space between last and next st; rep from * 3 times more, join with a slip st in first ch-5 sp.
**RND 3** [Sc, hdc, dc, 2 tr, dc, hdc, sc] in each ch-5 loop around, join with a slip st to first sc. Fasten off.

**RND 4** Attach B between first and last st of any petals. *Ch 6, sc in same st, ch 8, sc in same st, ch 6, sc in same sp, ch 4, working behind petals, sc in sp between next petal; rep from * 3 times more, join with a slip st to first ch of beg ch-6. Fasten off.
**RND 5** Attach D in any ch-8 lp. Ch 4 (counts as ch 1, 1 dc), [dc, ch 1, 2 dc] in same lp, *ch 2, dc in next ch-6 lp, ch 2, tr in center tip of next petal, ch 2, dc in next ch-6 lp, ch 2, [2 dc, ch 1, 2 dc] in next ch-8 lp; rep from * twice more, ch 2, dc in next ch-6 lp, ch 2, tr in center tip of next petal, ch 2, dc in next ch-6 lp, ch 2, join with a slip st to top of beg ch-4.
**RND 6** Sl st in first 2 dc, ch 2, *[dc, ch 2, dc] into next ch 2 sp, ch 2, [sc into next ch-2 sp, ch 2] 4 times; rep from * 3 times, join with a slip st to first dc. Fasten off.

## TOP

### CONNECT FLOWER MOTIFS

With RS facing of first motif, attach D with a slip st to any corner ch-2 sp. Ch 3 (counts as 1 dc), work 3 dc in each ch-3 sp across to next corner, dc in corner ch-2 sp. Place 2nd motif over first, with RS together, and insert hook through corner dc of motif 1 and in corresponding corner ch-2 sp of motif 2 and sc, *insert hook through next dc of motif 1 and in next ch-3 sp of motif 2 and sc, [insert hook through next dc of motif 1 and in same ch-3 sp of motif 2 and sc] twice more; rep from * to corner, insert hook through corner dc of motif 1 and in corresponding corner ch-2 sp of motif 2 and sc. Fasten off.

Rep for rem 2 motifs.

## LEFT UPPER BODICE AND SHOULDER

With RS facing, attach D with a slip st to right top corner of 2 connected motifs.

**ROW 1** Ch 5 (counts as 1 dc, ch 2), 4 dc in each ch-3 sp across to next corner, turn.

**ROW 2** Ch 3, skip first 5 dc, *2 dc in each of next 2 sts, skip next 2 dc; rep from * twice more, 2 dc in each of next 2 sts, skip next dc, dc in 3rd ch of beg ch-5, turn.

**ROW 3** Ch 3 (counts as 1 dc), skip first 2 dc, *2 dc in each of next 2 sts, skip next 2 dc; rep from * twice more, 2 dc in next dc, turn.

**ROW 4** Ch 3, skip first 3 dc, *2 dc in each of next 2 sts, skip next 2 dc; rep from * once more, 2 dc in each of next 2 sts, dc in top of beg ch-3, turn.

**ROW 5** Ch 3 (counts as 1 dc), skip first 2 dc, 2 dc in next st, skip next 2 dc, 2 dc in each of next 2 sts, skip next 2 sts, 2 dc in next st, turn.

**ROW 6** Ch 3, skip first 3 dc, 2 dc in each of next 2 sts, skip next 2

dc, 2 dc in next st, dc in top of beg ch-3, turn.

**ROW 7** Ch 3 (counts as 1 dc), skip first 4 sts, 2 dc in each of next 2 sts, dc in next dc, turn.

**ROW 8** Ch 3, skip first 2 dc, 2 dc in each of next 2 sts, skip next dc, dc in top of beg ch-3. Fasten off.

## LEFT FRONT SIDE EDGE

With RS facing, attach D with a slip st to bottom side corner of motif.

**ROW 1** Ch 3 (counts as 1 dc), dc into same corner ch-2 sp, *4 dc in next ch-3 sp; rep from * to top right corner of left bodice, turn.

**ROW 2** Ch 3 (counts as 1 dc), skip first dc, *2 dc in each of next 2 dc, skip next 2 dc; rep from * to last 2 sts, dc in top of beg ch-3, turn.

**ROW 3** Rep row 2. Fasten off.

## RIGHT UPPER BODICE AND SHOULDER

With RS facing, attach D with a slip st to right top corner of rem 2 connected motifs.

**ROW 1** Ch 5 (counts as 1 dc, ch 2), 4 dc in each ch-3 sp across to next corner, turn.

**ROW 2** Ch 3, skip first dc, *2 dc in each of next 2 sts, skip next 2 dc; rep from * twice more, 2 dc in each of next 2 sts, skip next dc, dc next st, turn.

**ROW 3** Ch 3 (counts as 1 dc), skip first 3 dc, 2 dc in next st, skip next 2 dc, *2 dc in each of next 2 sts, skip next 2 dc; rep from * once more, 2 dc in next dc, skip next dc, dc in top of beg ch-3, turn.

**ROW 4** Ch 3, skip first 2 dc, *2 dc in each of next 2 sts, skip next 2 dc; rep from * twice more, dc in next st, turn.

**ROW 5** Ch 3 (counts as 1 dc), skip first 3 dc, 2 dc in next st, skip next 2 dc, 2 dc in each of next 2 sts, skip next 2 sts, 2 dc in next st, dc in top of beg ch-3, turn.

**ROW 6** Ch 3, skip first dc, 2 dc in each of next st, skip next 2 dc, 2 dc in each of next 2 sts, skip next 2 dc, dc in next st, turn.

**ROW 7** Ch 3 (counts as 1 dc), skip first 2 sts, 2 dc in each of next 2 sts, skip next 2 dc, dc in next dc, turn.

**ROW 8** Ch 3, skip first 2 dc, 2 dc in each of next 2 sts, dc in next st. Fasten off.

## RIGHT FRONT SIDE EDGE

With RS facing, attach D with a slip st to top left corner of right bodice.

**ROW 1** Ch 3 (counts as 1 dc), dc into same corner ch-2 sp, *4 dc in next ch-3 sp; rep from * to bottom left corner of motifs, turn.

**ROW 2** Ch 3 (counts as 1 dc), skip first dc, *2 dc in each of next 2 dc, skip next 2 dc; rep from * to last 2 sts, dc in top of beg ch-3, turn.

**ROW 3** Rep row 2. Fasten off. Sew shoulder seams.

## BACK

With D, ch 31.

**ROW 1** Dc in 5th ch from hook (counts as 1 dc, ch 2), *2 dc in each of next 2 ch, skip next 2 ch; rep from * to last 3 ch, 2 dc in each

of next 2 ch, dc in last ch, turn.

**ROW 2** Ch 3 (counts as 1 dc), skip first 2 dc, 2 dc in each of next 2 sts, skip next 2 dc; rep from * to last 4 sts, 2 dc in each of next 2 sts, skip next dc, dc in top of beg ch-3, turn.

**ROWS 3–6** Rep row 2.

**ROW 7** Rep row 2, ch 5, turn.

## ARMHOLE SHAPING

**ROW 8** Dc in 5th ch from hook (counts as 1 dc, ch 2), *2 dc in each of next 2 sts, skip next 2 dc; rep from * to last 4 sts, 2 dc in each of next 2 sts, skip next dc, dc in top of beg ch-3, ch 5, turn.

**ROW 9** Dc in 5th ch from hook (counts as 1 dc, ch 2), *2 dc in each of next 2 sts, skip next 2 dc; rep from * to last 4 sts, 2 dc in each of next 2 sts, skip next dc, dc in top of beg ch-3, turn.

## LOWER BACK

**ROWS 10–26** Ch 3 (counts as 1 dc), skip first 2 dc, 2 dc in each of next 2 sts, skip next 2 dc; rep from * to last 4 sts, 2 dc in each of next 2 sts, skip next dc, dc in top of beg ch-3, turn. Fasten off. Sew front/back side seams to underarm.

## SLEEVES

With RS facing, attach D with a slip st in center of underarm seam.

**RND 1** Working into end sts of front/back, work 4 dc in each end st around, join with a slip st to first dc.

**RNDS 2 AND 3** Skip first dc, *2 dc in each of next 2 sts, skip next 2 dc; rep from * to last dc, skip last dc, join with a slip st to first dc.

**RND 4** Skip first dc, 2 dc in next st, *skip next 2 dc, 2 dc in each of next 2 sts; rep from * to last 5 dc, 2 dc in next st, join with a slip st to first dc.

**RNDS 5–8** Skip first dc, 2 dc in next st, skip next dc, *2 dc in each of next 2 sts, skip next 2 dc; rep from * to last 5 sts, 2 dc in next 2 sts, skip next dc, 2 dc in next st, join with a slip st to first dc. Fasten off.

## FINISHING
### COLLAR

With RS facing, attach A with a slip st to right upper bodice at neck edge of first row worked.

**ROW 1** Ch 1, 3 hdc in each sp and 1 hdc in each st to corresponding st on left front, turn.

**ROW 2** Ch 1, sc in each hdc across, turn.

**ROW 3** Ch 1, hdc in each sc across. Fasten off.
Sew snap to ends of collar.

## CAPRIS
### LEGS (MAKE 2)

With A, ch 44. Work twin V-st for a total of 15 rows, changing yarn color every row as follows: A, C, D.
Fold each leg in half lengthwise, and with RS tog sew leg seam. Turn to RS. Holding seams tog, sew crotch (4 sts each side of seam front to back). Fasten off.

### LEG JOINING

Keeping continuity of stripe sequence, attach next color to back center of leg opening and cont in twin V-st across both legs, join with a slip st to top of beg ch-3. Work a further 11 rnds in pat, keeping stripe sequence. Fasten off.

### BELT

With A, ch 4. Join with sl st in first ch to form a ring.

**RND 1** Sc in each ch around. Rep rnd 1 until piece measures 20"/51cm. Fasten off. Weave cord belt through spaces between 4 twin V-st clusters around top of capris.

### CLUTCH

Work rnds 1–6 of flower motif, substituting C for A. Set aside. With D, ch 33. Work in twin V-st pat until piece measures 3"/7.5cm. Fasten off. Fold in half and sew sides together. Sew snap to inside at center. Match two opposite corners of flower motif to top of bag at side seams. Tack back section to bag, leaving front section free for clutch front flap. ✿

# Checkmate

Red roses at the waist and black beading on the bodice and matching clutch make a winning statement.

## MATERIALS

- 1 1¾oz/50g ball (each approx 136yd/124m) of Rowan/Westminster Fibers *Pure Wool DK* (superwash wool) each in #625 black (A) and #2 white (B) ( 3 )
- One each sizes B/1 and G/6 (2.25 and 4mm) hooks OR SIZE TO OBTAIN GAUGE
- Perles De Verre black glass beads (230 pieces)
- Two ⅜"/10mm black buttons (JHB 93266 used in sample)
- 5 purchased red roses
- ⅛"/3mm-wide red ribbon, 1yd/1m long
- 1 snap (for clutch)

## GAUGE

16 sts and 16 rows = 4"/10cm over dc using size G/6 (4mm) hook. *Take time to check gauge.*

## STITCH GLOSSARY

**DC2TOG** [Yo, insert hook and draw up a lp, yo and draw through 2 lps on hook] twice, yo and draw through all 3 lps on hook.

## BASIC TUNISIAN STITCH

Chain number of sts in pat.
**ROW 1** Insert hook into 2nd chain from hook/st, yo, draw lp through and leave on hook. *Insert hook into next ch/st, yo, draw lp through and leave on hook; rep from * to end. Do *not* turn.
**ROW 2** Reverse: yo, draw through 1 lp, *yo, draw through 2 lps; rep from * until only 1 loop remains on hook. Do *not* turn.

## DRESS

### BACK SKIRT

With size G/6 (4mm) hook and A, ch 25.
**ROW 1** Sc in 2nd ch from hook and each ch to end of ch, turn—24 sts.
**ROW 2 (RS)** Ch 2, dc in each st across, turn.
**ROWS 3–12** Rep row 2.
**ROWS 13 AND 14** Ch 1, sl st in each st across. Break A and join B.

### BACK TOP

**ROWS 1 AND 2** With size G/6 (4mm) hook and B, work in Tunisian st across—24 sts.

### RIGHT SIDE BACK AND SHOULDER

**ROW 3** Work in Tunisian st across first 12 sts, turn, leaving rem sts unworked.
**ROWS 4–7** Working on first 12 sts only, continue in Tunisian st.
**ROW 8** Cont in Tunisian st across first 6 sts, turn, leaving rem sts unworked.
**ROWS 9 AND 10** Working on first 6 sts only, cont in Tunisian st. Fasten off.

### LEFT SIDE BACK AND SHOULDER

**ROW 1** With size G/6 (4mm) hook and RS facing, attach B to rem 12 sts and work in Tunisian st across last 12 sts.

**ROW 2** Cont in Tunisian st over 12 sts, ch 5 for button lp.

**ROWS 3–5** Cont in Tunisian st across, working ch-5 button lp at center back on last row.

**ROWS 6–8** Working on last 6 sts only, cont in Tunisian st. Fasten off.

### FRONT SKIRT

Work as given for back skirt.

### FRONT TOP

**ROWS 1–8** With size G/6 (4mm) hook and B, skip first st, work in Tunisian st across next 22 sts, leaving last st unworked—22 sts.

### LEFT SIDE FRONT AND SHOULDER

**ROW 9** Work in Tunisian st across first 6 sts, turn, leaving rem sts unworked.

**ROWS 10 AND 11** Working on first 6 sts only, cont in Tunisian st. Fasten off.

### RIGHT SIDE FRONT AND SHOULDER

**ROW 1** With RS facing, skip next 10 sts for center front. With size G/6 (4mm) hook, attach B to rem 6 sts and work in Tunisian st across last 6 sts. Fasten off.

**ROWS 2 AND 3** Working on last 6 sts only, cont in Tunisian st. Fasten off.

Sew front and back skirt side seams. Sew shoulder seams.

### SLEEVES

With size G/6 (4mm) hook and RS facing, attach B to right underarm side seam.

**RND 1 (RS)** Ch 2, work 32 dc evenly around armhole opening, join with a sl st to first dc.

**RND 2** Ch 2, dc2tog, dc in each st around to last 2 dc, dc2tog, join with a sl st to first dc—30 sts.

**RND 3** Ch 1, sl st in each st around, join with a sl st to first st.

**RND 4** Ch 2, dc tbl in each st around, join with a sl st to first dc.

**RNDS 5 AND 6** Rep row 4. Fasten off.

Rep for left sleeve.

### FINISHING

Fold last row of dc to inside of sleeve and whipstitch in place. Sew beads to front of dress top. Sew buttons to right back top opposite button loops. Using photo as a guide, sew purchased roses to front. Weave ribbon under the roses at waistline and tie into bow.

### CLUTCH

With size B/1 (2.25mm) hook and B, ch 21.

Work in Tunisian st for 12 rows. Fasten off.

Fold bottom up halfway to center of piece. Attach A to left corner of bag opening, working through both layers, work 1 row sc evenly down side, across bottom edge and up right side, then continue across opening single edge and around flap edge. Sew beads on front side of flap and sew snap for closure. ✿

# Go-go Girl

A matching vest, hat, and bag crocheted in fabulous fur will have her feeling groovy.

**MATERIALS**
- 1 3½oz/100g ball (each approx 65yd/59m) of Trendsetter Yarns *La Furla* (nylon) in #27 grape (4)
- Size I/9 (5.5mm) hook OR SIZE TO OBTAIN GAUGE
- 7"/18cm link bracelet (optional, for purse handle)
- Stitch markers

**GAUGE**
18 sts and 12 rows = 4"/10cm over dc using size I/9 (5.5mm) hook. *Take time to check gauge.*

**NOTE**
Vest is worked in one piece from lower back over shoulders to lower front.

**VEST**
BACK
Ch 23.
**ROW 1 (RS)** Dc in 2nd ch from hook and in each ch across, ch 2, turn—22 dc.
**ROW 2** Dc in each dc to end of row, ch 2, turn.
Rep row 2 until piece measures 4½"/11.5cm from beg, end with a WS row.

RIGHT FRONT
**ROW 1 (RS)** Dc in next 9 dc, ch 2, turn, leaving rem sts unworked—9 sts.
**ROW 2** Dc in each dc to end of row, ch 2, turn.
Rep row 2 for 6½"/16.5cm. Fasten off.

LEFT FRONT
With RS facing, sk next 4 dc for back neck, attach yarn with a sl st to next dc and work 1 dc in each dc to end of row—9 sts.
**ROW 2** Dc in each dc to end of row, ch 2, turn.
Rep row 2 for 6½"/16.5cm. Fasten off.

**FINISHING**
Fold fronts and back together, matching first row of back with last row of fronts. Starting at lower edge, sew side seams, leaving last 2"/5cm open on each side for armholes.

**HAT**
Ch 3. Join with a sl st into first ch to form a ring. Place marker for beg of rnd.
**RND 1** 8 dc into ring, join with a sl st to top of first dc—8 sts.
**RND 2** Work 2 dc in each dc to end of rnd, join with a sl st to top of first dc—16 sts.
**RND 3** *Dc in next st, 2 dc in next st; rep from * to end of rnd, join with a sl st to top of first dc—24 sts.
**RND 4** *Dc in next 2 sts, 2 dc in next st; rep from * to end of rnd, join with a sl st to top of first dc—32 sts.
**RND 5** *Dc in next 3 sts, 2 dc in next st; rep from * to end of rnd, join with a sl st to top of first dc—40 sts.
**RNDS 6–13** Dc in each st to end of rnd, join with a sl st to top of first dc.
Fasten off. Turn hat RS out.

## PURSE

Ch 18. Join with a sl st into first ch to form a ring. Place marker for beg of rnd.

**RND 1** Dc into each ch to end of rnd, join with a sl st to top of first dc.

**RND 2** Dc into each dc to end of rnd, join with a sl st to top of first dc.

Rep rnd 2 until piece measures 2"/5cm from beg. Fasten off.

## HANDLE

Fold bag in half and mark side edges at top of purse. Using a 7"/18cm link bracelet or a crocheted chain, attach handle to top of purse at markers. ✿

# Budding Beauty

Nothing says springtime more than a vibrantly colored floral top, ruffled skirt, and sun hat.

## MATERIALS

- 1 2.8oz/80g package of 8 skeins (each 28yd/26m) of Lion Brand Yarn *Bonbons* (cotton) in #601-630 beach (2)
- One each sizes C/2 (2.75mm) and D/3 (3.25mm) hooks OR SIZE TO OBTAIN GAUGE
- Stitch markers
- 3 small snaps

One decorative button (for hat)

## GAUGE

20 sts and 12 rows = 4"/10cm over dc using size C/2 (2.75mm) hook. *Take time to check gauge.*

## NOTES

**1)** Skirt is worked from the waist down.
**2)** Colors used are white (A), turquoise (B), yellow (C), black (D), red (E), and purple (F).
**3)** Hat in photo is shown worn over a wide-brimmed straw hat.

## TOP
### FLOWER MEDALLION/FRONT

With C/2 (2.75mm) hook and E, ch 8. Join with sl st in first ch to form a ring.

**RND 1** 18 sc in ring, join with a sl st to first sc. Break E and join F.
**RND 2** With F, ch 6, sk 1 sc, dc in next sc, *ch 4, sk next sc, dc in next sc; rep from * 7 more times, join with a sl st to 3rd ch of beg ch-6.
**RND 3** [Sc, hdc, 2 dc, hdc, sc] in beg ch-6 sp, *[sc, hdc, 2 dc, hdc, sc] in next ch-4 sp; rep from * 7 more times, join with a sl st to beg sc—9 petals.

**RND 4** Working behind petals, *ch 6, sl st to center of next petal; rep from * behind each petal around, join with a sl st to beg ch 6. Break F and join B.
**RNDS 5 AND 6** With B, rep rnds 3 and 4. Break B and join C.
**RND 7** With C, [sc, hdc, 2 dc, hdc, sc] in beg ch-6 sp, *[sc, hdc, 2 dc, hdc, sc] in next ch-4 sp; rep from * 7 more times, join with a sl st to beg sc.
**RND 8** Working behind petals, *ch 8, sl st to center of next petal; rep from * behind each petal around, join with a sl st to beg ch 8. Break C and join A.
**RND 9** With A, *[sc, ch 3, sc] in next ch-8 sp, ch 3; rep from * around, join with a sl st to first sc.
**RND 10** *[Sc, ch 1, sc] in next ch-3 sp, ch 2; rep from * around, join with a sl st to first sc.
**RND 11** *Sc in next ch-1 sp, ch 1, sc in next ch-2 sp, ch 2; rep from * around, join with a sl st to first sc. Break A and join D.
**RND 12** With D, *sc in next ch-2 sp, ch 2; rep from * around; join with a sl st to first sc. Turn.
**RND 13** Place marker for first strap, *sc in next ch-2 sp, sc in next sc; rep from * 17 times more. Fasten off.

## RIGHT STRAP

With RS facing, attach A with a sl st into ch-2 sp at marker for first strap, sc in same ch-2 sp, ch 2, [sc in next ch-2 sp, ch 2] twice, sc in next ch-2 sp, turn.

**ROW 1** [Ch 2, sc in next ch-2 sp] 3 times, turn.

**ROWS 2–10** Rep row 1. Fasten off.

## LEFT STRAP

With RS facing, skip next 4 sc's to left of right strap. Attach A with a sl st in next ch-2 sp, sc in same ch-2 sp, ch 2, [sc in next ch-2 sp, ch 2] twice, sc in next ch-2 sp, turn.

**ROW 1** [Ch 2, sc in ch-2 sp] 3 times, turn.

**ROWS 2–10** Rep row 1.

**JOINING ROW (WS)** [Ch 2, sc in next ch-2 sp] 3 times, ch 13 for back neck, sl st into last sc of right strap, [sc in next ch-2 sp, ch 2] twice, sc in last ch-2 sp, turn.

**ROW 12** Ch 2, [sc in next ch-2 sp, ch 2] twice, [sc in next ch, ch 2, skip next 2 ch] 4 times, sc in last ch, ch 2, [sc in next ch-2 sp, ch 2] twice, sc in last ch-2 sp, turn.

**ROW 13** Ch 2, *sc in next ch-2 sp, ch 2; rep from * to last ch-2 sp, sc in last ch-2 sp, turn. Break A and join C.

**ROWS 14–16** With C, rep row 13. Break C and join B.

**ROW 17** With B, ch 2, join back to flower medallion/front with a sl st to 5th sc down from right shoulder strap join, ch 1, *sc in next ch-2 sp, ch 2; rep from * to last ch-2 sp, sc in last ch-2 sp, turn.

**ROW 18** Ch 2, *sc in next ch-2 sp, ch 2; rep from * to end of row, join with a sl st to next ch-2 sp of flower medallion/front, turn.

**ROW 19** Ch 2, *sc in next ch-2 sp, ch 2; rep from * to last ch-2 sp, sc in last ch-2 sp, turn.

**ROW 20** Ch 2, *sc in next ch-2 sp, ch 2; rep from * to end of row, join with a sl st to next ch-2 sp of flower medallion/front, turn.

**ROW 21** Ch 2, sc into last ch-2 of row 20, *ch 2, sc in next ch-2 sp; rep from * to end of row, turn. Break B and join F.

**ROW 22** With F, ch 2, *sc in next ch-2 sp, ch 2; rep from * to end of row, join with a sl st to next ch-2 sp of flower medallion/front, turn.

**ROW 23** Ch 2, sc into last ch-2 of row 22, *ch 2, sc in next ch-2 sp; rep from * to end of row, turn.

**ROWS 24 AND 25** Rep rows 22 and 23. Break F and join E.

**ROWS 26–29** With E, rep rows 22 and 23 twice.

**ROW 30** Rep row 22. Fasten off.

## LEFT SIDE CLOSURE FLAP

**NEXT ROW** With RS facing, attach E with a sl st to sc on last row of medallion to match last row of back, [ch 1, sc in next sc] 4 times, with F, [ch 1, sc in next sc] 4 times, with B, [ch 1, sc in next sc] 4 times, turn.

**ROW 2** With B, ch 2, [sc in next ch-1 sp, ch 1] 4 times, with F, [sc in next ch-1 sp, ch 1] 4 times, with E, [sc in next ch-1 sp, ch 1] 4 times, turn.

**ROW 3** With E, ch 2, [sc in next ch-1 sp, ch 1] 4 times, with F, [sc in next ch-1 sp, ch 1] 4 times, with B, [sc in next ch-1 sp, ch 1] 4 times, turn.

**ROW 4** Rep row 2. Fasten off. Sew 2 snaps to WS of left side closure flap and coordinating position on left back side edge.

## SKIRT

With D/3 (3.25m) hook and E, ch 45, turn.

**ROW 1** Hdc in 2nd ch from hook and in each ch across, turn— 44 sts.

**ROW 2** Ch 1, dc in each hdc across, turn.

**ROW 3** Ch 2, dc in each dc across, turn. Break E and join D.

**ROW 4** With D, ch 2, dc in each dc across, turn.

**ROWS 5–8** Ch 2, dc in each dc across, turn. Break D and join A.

**ROW 9** With C/2 (2.75mm) hook and A, ch 1, sc in each st across, turn.

**ROWS 10 AND 11** Ch 1, sc in each st across, turn. Break A and join B.

**ROWS 12–14** With B, rep rnds 9–11. Break B and join F.

### Wear on its own or over a wide-brim hat!

**ROW 15** With F, ch 1, sc in each st across, turn.

**ROWS 16–18** Ch 1, sc in each sc across, turn.

**ROW 19** Ch 4 (counts as 1 tr), 1 tr in first sc, 3 tr in next sc, *2 tr in next sc, 3 tr in next sc; rep from * across. Fasten off.

**FINISHING**

Sew center back seam, leaving last 1½"/4cm to waist edge open.

Sew snap fastener to waist edge of back opening.

**HAT**

With D/3 (3.25mm) hook and F, ch 63.

**ROW 1** Hdc in 2nd ch from hook and in each ch across, turn—62 sts. Break F and join B.

**ROW 2** With B, dc in each hdc across, turn. Break B and join C.

**ROWS 3 AND 4** With C, ch 2, dc in each dc across, turn.

**ROW 5** Ch 2, dc in each dc to last 8 sts, turn, leaving last 8 sts unworked for flap—54 sts. Break C and join E.

**ROWS 6 AND 7** With E, ch 2, dc in each dc across, turn. Break E and join A.

**ROW 8** With A, ch 2, *dc2tog; rep from * across, turn—27 sts.

**ROW 9** Ch 2 dc in first dc, *dc2tog; rep from * across, turn—14 sts. Break A and join F.

**ROW 10** With F, ch 2, *dc2tog; rep from * across, turn—7 sts.

**ROW 11** Ch 2, dc in first dc, [dc2tog] 3 times, turn—4 sts. Fasten off.

**FINISHING**

Sew seam from top of hat to flap.

**RUFFLE**

With size D/3 (3.25mm) hook, join F with a slip st to 24th ch along beg ch, ch 4 (counts as 1 tr), tr into same st as sl st, [3 tr in next ch, 2 tr in next ch] 20 times, working through both layers along flap, 3 tr in next ch. Fasten off.

**FLAP EDGING**

With size C/2 (2.75mm) hook, join E with a sl st to seam. Work rev sc over rem 8 sts for flap, work 7 st rev sc evenly along side edge of flap, work 2 sts rev sc in first 2 ch of beg ch. Fasten off. Place flap over main hat and sew in position. Sew button to flap, using photo as a guide. ✿

# Arctic Angel

A soft-as-snow pink coat with white pompom ties and matching bag are the ultimate cold-weather chic.

## MATERIALS

- 1 1¾oz/50g skein (each approx 137yd/125m) of Lion Brand Yarn *Jamie* (acrylic) in #881-100 angel white (A) ⓷
- 2 1¾oz/50g skeins (each approx 64yd/58m) of Lion Brand Yarn *Fun Fur* (polyester) in #320-101 soft pink (B) ⓷
- One each sizes C/2 (2.75mm) and D/3 (3.25mm) hooks OR SIZE TO OBTAIN GAUGE
- Stitch marker
- 2 cotton balls
- Five ½"/1.5cm buttons (JHB #40200 used in sample)

## GAUGE

10 sts and 6 rows = 4"/10cm over dc using B and size D/3 (3.25mm) hook. *Take time to check gauge.*

## SINGLE CROCHET RIBBING (SC RIB)

Ch the required number of sts.
**ROW 1** Sc in 2nd ch from hook and in each ch across, turn.
**ROW 2** Ch 1, working in back lps only, sc in each sc across, turn.
Rep row 2 for sc rib.

## NOTES

**1)** Garment is made in one piece (including hood) and is worked sideways starting at center fronts and ending at center back.
**2)** Sleeves are worked separately and sewn into armhole opening.

## COAT

### FRONTS AND HOOD

With size C/2 (2.75mm) hook and A, ch 143.
**ROW 1 (WS)** Sc in 2nd ch and in each ch across—142 sc, turn. Cut A and attach B.
**ROWS 2–5** With B, ch 1, sc in each sc to end of row, turn. Do not cut B, attach A at end of last row.
**ROW 6** With A, ch 1, sc in each sc to end of row, do *not* turn.
**ROW 7** With A, ch 1, rev sc in each st to end of row, do *not* turn. Cut A, pick up B.

**ROWS 8–11** Rep rows 2–5. Do not cut B, attach A at end of last row.
**ROW 12** With A, ch 1, sc in next 35 sts, ch 12, sk 12 sts (left armhole), sc in next 48 sts, ch 12, sk 12 sts (right armhole), sc in next 35 sts.
**ROW 13** With A, rev sc in each st, including 12 ch sts for armholes—142 sc. Cut A, pick up B.

### BACK

**ROWS 14–25** With size D/3 (3.25mm) hook, work rows 2–7 twice. Cut A, pick up B.
Fold hood in half with WS together. Measure 4"/10cm down from center top and, using A, sew rev sc rows tog for 4"/10cm to form center back hood seam.
**ROW 26** With B, ch 1, sc in each st to 2 sts before center back hood seam, sc2tog, place marker, sc2tog, sc in each st to end of row, turn.
**ROWS 27–31** Ch 1, sc in each st to 2 sts before marker, sc2tog, slip marker (sm), sc2tog, sc in each st to end of row, turn. Do not cut B, attach A at end of last row.

**ROW 32** With A, sc in each st to 2 sts before marker, sc2tog, sm, sc2tog, sc in each st to end of row, do not turn.

**ROW 33** With A, ch 1, rev sc in each sc to 2 sts before marker, rev sc2tog, sm, rev sc2tog, rev sc in each sc to end of row, do not turn. Cut A, pick up B.

**ROWS 34-41** With B, ch 1, sc in each st to 2 sts before marker, sc2tog, slip marker (sm), sc2tog, sc in each st to end of row, turn. Do not cut B, attach A at end of last row.

**ROW 42** With A, sc in each st to 2 sts before marker, sc2tog, sm, sc2tog, sc in each st to end of row, do not turn.

**ROW 43** With A, ch 1, rev sc in each sc to 2 sts before marker, rev sc2tog, sm, rev sc2tog, rev sc in each sc to end of row, do not turn.
Cut A, pick up B.

**ROW 44** With B, rep row 34 until no sts rem. Fasten off.

LEFT FRONT EDGING

With RS facing and A, attach yarn with a sl st to coat bottom edge.

**ROW 1** Ch 1, rev sc in next 48 sts, do *not* turn.

**ROW 2** Ch 1, sc in each st to end of row, do *not* turn.

**ROW 3** Ch 1, rev sc in next 48 sts. Fasten off.

RIGHT FRONT EDGING

With RS facing and A, attach yarn with a sl st to 48th st from lower edge.

**ROWS 1, 3, AND 5** Ch 1, rev sc in next 48 sts, do *not* turn.

**ROWS 2 AND 4** Ch 1, sc in each st to end of row, do *not* turn. Place 4 buttons evenly spaced and mark placement.

**ROW 6 (BUTTON LOOP ROW)** Ch 1, sc in first 10 sts, *ch 3 (lp made), sc in next 11 sts; rep from * twice more, ch 3 (lp made), sc to end of row, do *not* turn.

**ROW 7** Ch 1, rev sc in each st and 3 rev sc in each ch-3 space to end of row. Fasten off. Sew buttons to left front edging opposite side to line up with ch-3 lps.

SLEEVES (MAKE 2)

With size C/2 (2.75mm) hook and A, ch 24.
Work 18 rows sc rib st (9 ribs), turn work 90 degrees clockwise.

SLEEVE TOP

**ROW 1 (RS)** Ch 1, work 22 sc evenly across short side of sleeve, do *not* turn.

**ROW 2** Ch 1, work rev sc over 22 sts, do *not* turn.

**ROW 3** Ch 1, work sc in next 22 sts, do *not* turn.
Rep last 2 rows once more.
Fasten off.

FINISHING

Fold sleeves in half, bringing long sides together. With RS of coat facing and size C/2 (2.75mm) hook, position rev sc edge of sleeve to fit in armhole space. Starting at front underarm edge and holding both pieces tog, rev sc through both pieces around to back underarm, and then sl st down sleeve to close. Rep for other sleeve.

POMPOM (MAKE 2)

With size C/2 (2.75mm) hook and A, ch 2.

**RND 1** Work 3 sc in 2nd ch, join with a sl st to first sc.

**RND 2** Sc in each st, join with a sl st to first sc.
Rep rnd 2 for 1"/2.5cm, stuff ball with cotton, and sl st closed. Fasten off.

TIE

With size C/2 (2.75mm) hook and A, ch 50.

**ROW 1** Sl st in 2nd ch and each ch to end. Fasten off. Thread tie through sts at neckline of coat. Attach one pompom to each tie end.

edge and cont with sl st down right side and across bottom. Cut yarn.

BUTTON LOOP
Attach A to back top edge, centering work over middle 3 dc.
**ROW 1** Ch 1, sc in next 3 sts, turn. Rep last row 5 times more, leaving a loop on last sc for button closure. Attach button to front top center.

FINISHING
HANDLE
With C/2 (2.75mm) hook and A, ch 25.
**ROW 1** Sc in 2nd ch from hook and in each ch across. Cut A and join B.
**ROW 2** Ch 1, sc in each sc across. Cut yarn and fasten off. With A, sew ends of handle to each side of handbag. ✿

HANDBAG
With size D/3 (3.25mm) hook and B, ch 40.
**ROW 1** Dc in 2nd ch from hook and in each ch across, turn—39 sts.
**ROWS 2–8** Ch 2, dc in each dc to end of row, turn. Do not cut yarn.
Fold left side over to right side

Extras
and
Resources

# A Little Bit of Bling

It's fun and easy to make jewelry that matches your doll's outfits!

**GO-GO BRACELET**

A big-girl bracelet or necklace can be wrapped multiple times.
*See page 105.*

**FIESTA CHOKER**

A personalized charm bracelet makes a fun necklace.
*See page 31.*

**SOUTHERN BELLE BRACELET**

A broken chain can be repurposed with a purchased clasp.
*See page 27.*

**AFTERNOON TEA NECKLACE**

Use two beaded bracelets as a multistrand necklace.
*See page 15.*

**CIRCUS OF COLOR BRACELET**

String some beads on elastic thread long enough to stretch over the doll's hand.
*See page 55.*

**NIGHT AT THE OPERA NECKLACE**

A delicate bracelet can make a big statement around a doll's neck.
*See page 35.*

# Sweets for the Sweet

Bake some tasty treats as sweet as your dolls!

## CANDIED FRUIT COOKIES

- ¼ lb butter
- ¼ lb light brown sugar
- 1 egg
- ¼ lb golden raisins
- ¼ lb walnuts, finely chopped
- ¼ lb red and green candied cherries, chopped
- ¼ lb candied pineapple, chopped
- 3 oz shredded coconut
- 1 C flour, plus additional ¼ C to coat fruit
- ¼ tsp baking soda
- ½ tsp vanilla

✿ Preheat oven to 375°. Combine butter, brown sugar, egg, and vanilla in a large mixing bowl. Combine baking soda and 1C flour and add gradually to butter mixture. Fold in raisins and nuts. In small bowl, coat candied cherries and pineapple with ¼C flour. Fold coated fruit into batter.

Drop teaspoons of batter onto parchment paper on a cookie sheet. Bake 8–10 min.

Makes approx. 2 dozen cookies.

## SHORTBREAD SWEETHEART COOKIES

- ¾ C butter
- ¼ C sugar
- 2 C flour
- Food coloring (optional)
- Powdered sugar

✿ Mix butter and sugar together until thoroughly combined. Add flour gradually until mixed to form dough. Tint with food coloring if desired. Chill for 2 hours.

Preheat oven to 350°. Roll dough to ½" thick. Cut into shapes with heart-shaped cookie cutter, or desired shape. Place on ungreased cookie sheet or parchment paper. Bake for 20 min.; do not brown. Sprinkle with powdered sugar if desired.

Makes approx. 2 dozen cookies.

## CHEERY CHEERIOS COOKIES

- 4 C Cheerios
- 1 C salted peanuts
- 1 C shredded coconut
- 1 C sugar
- ½ C corn syrup
- 1 C heavy cream

✿ Combine Cheerios, peanuts, and coconut in a large greased mixing bowl.

Combine sugar, corn syrup, and cream in a saucepan. Cook over low heat, stirring until soft. (Mixture should form a ball when dropped in cold water.)

Pour syrup mixture over Cheerios mixture, blend well. Form small round patties and cool until firm.

Makes approx. 2 dozen cookies.

# Glossary and Techniques

## Abbreviations

| | |
|---|---|
| **APPROX** | approximately |
| **BEG** | begin; beginning; begins |
| **BPDC** | back post double crochet |
| **CH** | chain; chains |
| **CL** | cluster |
| **CONT** | continue; continuing |
| **DC** | double crochet |
| **DEC** | decrease; decreasing |
| **DTR** | double treble crochet |
| **FOLL** | follow(s) (ing) |
| **FPDC** | front post double crochet |
| **GRP(S)** | group(s) |
| **HDC** | half double crochet |
| **INC** | increase; increasing |
| **LP(S)** | loop(s) |
| **PAT(S)** | pattern(s) |
| **RS** | right side |
| **REM** | remain; remains; remaining |
| **REP** | repeat |
| **REVERSE** | sc reverse single crochet (aka crab stitch) |
| **RND(S)** | round(s) |
| **SC** | single crochet |
| **SC2TOG** | single crochet two together |
| **SK** | skip |
| **SL** | slip; slipping |
| **SL** | st slip stitch |
| **SP(S)** | space(s) |
| **ST(S)** | stitch(es) |
| **TBL** | through back loop |
| **T-CH** | turning chain |
| **TFL** | through front loop |
| **TOG** | together |
| **TR** | treble crochet |
| **TRTR** | triple treble crochet |
| **WS** | wrong side |
| **WORK EVEN** | Continue in pattern without increasing or decreasing (U.K.: work straight) |
| **YO** | yarn over hook. Making a new stitch by wrapping the yarn around the hook (U.K.: yoh) |
| **( )** | work instructions contained inside the parentheses into the stitch indicated |
| **[ ]** | rep instructions within brackets as many times as directed |
| **\*** | rep instructions following an asterisk as many times as indicated |

## Conversion Chart

| U.S. TERM | U.K./AUS TERM |
|---|---|
| **SL ST** (slip stitch) | **SC** (single crochet) |
| **SC** (single crochet) | **DC** (double crochet) |
| **HDC** (half double crochet) | **HTR** (half treble crochet) |
| **DC** (double crochet) | **TR** (treble crochet) |
| **TR** (treble crochet) | **DTR** (double treble crochet) |
| **DTR** (double treble crochet) | **TRIP TR OR TRTR** (triple treble crochet) |
| **TRTR** (triple treble crochet) | **QTR** (quadruple treble crochet) |
| **REV SC** (reverse single crochet) | **REV DC** (reverse double crochet) |
| **YO** (yarn over) | **YOH** (yarn over hook) |

# Standard Yarn Weight System

Categories of yarn, gauge ranges, and recommended needle and hook sizes

| Yarn Weight Symbol & Category Names | **0** Lace | **1** Super Fine | **2** Fine | **3** Light | **4** Medium | **5** Bulky | **6** Super Bulky |
|---|---|---|---|---|---|---|---|
| Type of Yarns in Category | Fingering 10 count crochet thread | Sock, Fingering, Baby | Sport, Baby | DK, Light Worsted | Worsted, Afghan, Aran | Chunky, Craft, Rug | Bulky, Roving |
| Knit Gauge Range* in Stockinette Stitch to 4 inches | 33–40** sts | 27–32 sts | 23–26 sts | 21–24 sts | 16–20 sts | 12–15 sts | 6–11 sts |
| Recommended Needle in Metric Size Range | 1.5–2.25 mm | 2.25–3.25 mm | 3.25–3.75 mm | 3.75–4.5 mm | 4.5–5.5 mm | 5.5–8 mm | 8 mm and larger |
| Recommended Needle U.S. Size Range | 000 to 1 | 1 to 3 | 3 to 5 | 5 to 7 | 7 to 9 | 9 to 11 | 11 and larger |
| Crochet Gauge* Ranges in Single Crochet to 4 inch | 32–42 double crochets** | 21–32 sts | 16–20 sts | 12–17 sts | 11–14 sts | 8–11 sts | 5–9 sts |
| Recommended Hook in Metric Size Range | Steel*** 1.6–1.4mm Regular hook 2.25 mm | 2.25–3.5 mm | 3.5–4.5 mm | 4.5–5.5 mm | 5.5–6.5 mm | 6.5–9 mm | 9 mm and larger |
| Recommended Hook U.S. Size Range | Steel*** 6, 7, 8 Regular hook B–1 | B–1 to E–4 | E–4 to 7 | 7 to I–9 | I–9 to K–10½ | K–10½ to M–13 | M–13 and larger |

* GUIDELINES ONLY: The above reflect the most commonly used gauges and needle or hook sizes for specific yarn categories.

** Lace weight yarns are usually knitted or crocheted on larger needles and hooks to create lacy, openwork patterns. Accordingly, a gauge range is difficult to determine. Always follow the gauge stated in your pattern.

*** Steel crochet hooks are sized differently from regular hooks--the higher the number, the smaller the hook, which is the reverse of regular hook sizing.

This Standards & Guidelines booklet and downloadable symbol artwork are available at: **YarnStandards.com**

# Crochet Hooks

| U.S. | METRIC |
|---|---|
| B/1 | 2.25MM |
| C/2 | 2.75MM |
| D/3 | 3.25MM |
| E/4 | 3.5MM |
| F/5 | 3.75MM |
| G/6 | 4MM |
| 7 | 4.5MM |
| H/8 | 5MM |
| I/9 | 5.5MM |
| J/10 | 6MM |
| K/10½ | 6.5MM |
| L/11 | 8MM |
| M/13 | 9MM |
| N/15 | 10MM |

## SKILL LEVELS FOR CROCHET

■□□□ **BEGINNER** - Ideal first project.

■■□□ **EASY** - Indicates basic stitches, minimal shaping and simple finishing.

■■■□ **INTERMEDIATE** - For crocheters with some experience. More intricate stitches, shaping and finishing.

■■■■ **EXPERIENCED** - For crocheters able to work patterns with complicated shaping and finishing.

# Embroidery Stitches

**FRENCH KNOT**

**LAZY DAISY STITCH**

**CROSS STITCH**

**STRAIGHT STITCH**

# Techniques

## Chain

**1.** Pass yarn over hook and catch with hook.

**2.** Draw yarn through loop on hook.

**3.** Repeat steps 1 and 2 to make chain.

## Single Crochet

**1.** Insert hook through top two loops of a stitch. Pass yarn over hook and draw up a loop—two loops on hook.

**2.** Pass yarn over hook and draw through both loops on hook.

**3.** Continue in the same way, inserting hook into each stitch.

## Double Crochet

**1.** Pass yarn over hook. Insert hook through top two loops of a stitch.

**2.** Pass yarn over hook and draw up a loop—three loops on hook.

**3.** Pass yarn over hook and draw it through first two loops on hook; pass yarn over hook and draw through remaining two loops. Continue in same way, inserting hook into each stitch.

# Yarn Resources

**AUNT LYDIA'S**
A Coats & Clark brand

**CASCADE YARNS**
1224 Andover Park East
Tukwila, WA 98188
www.cascadeyarns.com

**COATS & CLARK**
PO Box 12229
Greenville, SC 29612
tel: (800) 648-1479
www.coatsandclark.com

**DEBBIE BLISS**
Distributed by Knitting Fever
www.debbieblissonline.com

**DMC**
10 Basin Drive
Suite 130
Kearny, NJ 07032
Tel: (973) 589-0606
www.dmc-usa.com

**KNITTING FEVER (KFI)**
PO Box 336
315 Bayview Avenue
Amityville, NY 11701
www.knittingfever.com

**KNIT ONE, CROCHET TWO**
91 Tandberg Trail, Unit 6
Windham, ME 04062
Tel: (207) 892-9625
www.knitonecrochettoo.com

**KOIGU WOOL DESIGNS**
PO Box 158
Chatsworth, Ontario N0H1G0
Canada
Tel: (888) 765-WOOL (765-9665)
www.koigu.com

**LION BRAND YARN CO.**
34 West 15th Street
New York, NY 10011
www.lionbrand.com

**PLYMOUTH YARN CO.**
500 Lafayette Street
Bristol, PA 19007
Tel: (215) 788-0459
www.plymouthyarn.com

**PRESENCIA**
PO Box 2409
Evergreen, CO 80437
Tel: (866) 277-6364

**RED HEART LTD.**
A Coats & Clark brand
www.redheart.com

**SCHULANA**
Distributed by Skacel
Collection, Inc.

**SKACEL COLLECTION, INC.**
www.skacelknitting.com

**TAHKI•STACY CHARLES, INC.**
70-60 83rd Street, Building #12
Glendale, NY 11385
www.tahkistacycharles.com

**TRENDSETTER YARNS**
16745 Saticoy Street, Suite 101
Van Nuys, CA 91406
www.trendsetteryarns.com

**YARN RESOURCES IN THE UK AND EUROPE**

**GRIGNASCO KNITS**
Via Dante Alighieri n. 2
28075 Grignasco, Novara
Italy
Tel: +39 0163 4101
www.grignascoknits.it

**ROWAN YARNS**
Green Lane Mill
Holmfirth, West Yorkshire
HD9 2DX
England
Tel: +44 (0)1484 681881
www.knitrowan.com

Teacups, page 15
Hand-painted ceramics by
Sally Mara Sturman
www.sallymarasturman.com

# Project Index

## ACCESSORIES AND BAGS

Arctic Angel, 115 (bag)

Candy Couture, 90 (bag)

Checkmate, 103 (clutch)

Circus of Color, 59 (bag)

Cowl and Critters, 82–83 (cowl)

Give It a Whirl, 25 (purse)

Go-go Girl, 106 (purse)

Pretty as a Picture, 78 (purse)

**Royal Princess, 62 (purse)**

Slip into Sleepytime, 53 (slippers)

Walking on Sunshine, 100 (clutch)

Wildflower, 47–49 (scarf, mittens)

## BOTTOMS

Budding Beauty, 109–110 (skirt)

Fit for a Fiesta, 30 (skirt)

Get Your Kicks, 20 (pants)

Hip to Be Square, 42–43 (fabric skirt)

Pretty as a Picture, 75–77 (skirt)

**Walking on Sunshine, 100 (pants)**

## DÉCOR

Daisy Mays, 44–45 (flowers)

**Striped Safari, 66–70 (afghan)**

## DRESSES

Afternoon Tea, 14–17

Checkmate, 101–103

Circus of Color, 54–58

Dressed Up in Daisies, 64–65

Give It a Whirl, 22–25

**Let It Snow, 94–96**

Night at the Opera, A, 34–38

Royal Princess, 59–62

Wrapped in Ruffles, 79–81

**HATS AND HEADPIECES**

Budding Beauty, 110 (hat)

Candy Couture, 90 (hat)

Cowl and Critters, 82–86 (3 hats)

Floral Beauty, 92 (hat)

Get Your Kicks, 20 (visor)

Go-go Girl, 106 (hat)

Hip to Be Square, 42–43 (bandana)

Irish Eyes, 74 (hat)

Let It Snow, 96 (headband)

Royal Princess, 61–62 (crown)

**Wildflower, 47–49 (hat)**

**JACKETS, SHAWLS, AND ROBES**

Arctic Angel, 114–115 (coat)

Candy Couture, 87–90 (jacket)

Fit for a Fiesta, 33 (shawl)

Floral Beauty, 91–92 (poncho)

Get Your Kicks, 18–21 (jacket)

**Give It a Whirl, 25 (jacket)**

Irish Eyes, 71–74 (coat)

Night at the Opera, A 34–38 (shawl),

**Slip into Sleepytime, 51 53 (robe)**


**TOPS AND VESTS**

Budding Beauty, 107–110

Go-go Girl, 104

**Hip to Be Square, 39–43**

Southern Belle, 27–29

Pretty as a Picture, 75–77

Walking on Sunshine, 97–100

# Acknowledgments

This book could not exist without the talented and hardworking dolls at Sixth&Spring Books.

My thanks to…

Art Joinnides and Jay Stein, who keep all the dolls dancing.

Joy Aquilino, my wonderful, "getting it done" editor.

Diane Lamphron, art director, for her inspired work, which contributed so greatly to the lovely look of this book.

Jack Deutsch and his team. Jack's photography made the dolls come to life with his beautiful lighting and techniques. He can shoot a bagel and give it personality!

Johanna Levy, stylist, whose contributions to clothing, hair, etc. lent such panache.

Lisa Silverman, developmental editor, who knows how to get to the essence of the garments with her words.

Christina Behnke, yarn editor, who made sure each garment was made from the ideal yarn.

Trisha Malcolm and Carla Scott, who offer support, talent, and friendship, as always.

Stephanie Mrse and Sandi Prosser, tireless pattern writers and technical editors.

David Joinnides, just because he's as cute as a button.

My dear pal and crochet genius, Jo Brandon, who beautifully crocheted the bulk of the garments, and Eileen Curry and Nancy Henderson, who are always there for me.

Thanks to the generous folks at JHB International who supplied all the lovely buttons, and to all the yarn companies, who were so kind.

Many thanks to the Alexander Doll Company, a division of KLL Dolls, LLC, for contributing their beautiful dolls to be photographed.

My darling husband, Howard, who put up with 25 dolls (26, counting me) staring at him for months.

And, last but not least, a big thank you to the lovely little models who worked tirelessly for many long hours, without uttering a single negative word. ✿

**OTHER CROCHET AND KNITTING BOOKS BY NICKY EPSTEIN**

Cover Up with
Nicky Epstein

Crocheting on the Edge

Knitting a Kiss in
Every Stitch

Knitting Beyond
the Edge

Knitting on the Edge

Knitting Over the Edge

Knitting Never
Felt Better

Nicky Epstein
Crocheted Flowers

Nicky Epstein
Kints for Dolls

Nicky Epstein
Knitted Flowers

Nicky Epstein Knitting
in Tuscany

Nicky Epstein Knitting
on Top of the World

Nicky Epstein
The Essential Edgings
Collection

Nicky Epstein's
Signature Scarves

Nicky
Epstein
Books
an imprint of

sixth&spring
books

sixthandspringbooks.com

Let's go out and show off our new looks!